CLARITY
IN CRISIS

LEADERSHIP LESSONS FROM THE CIA

MARC POLYMEROPOULOS

FORMER SENIOR INTELLIGENCE OFFICER, CIA

CLARITY
IN CRISIS

LEADERSHIP LESSONS FROM THE CIA

HarperCollins
Leadership

An Imprint of HarperCollins

Published by HarperCollins Leadership, an imprint of HarperCollins Focus LLC.

Any internet addresses, phone numbers, or company or product information printed in this book are offered as a resource and are not intended in any way to be or to imply an endorsement by HarperCollins Leadership, nor does HarperCollins Leadership vouch for the existence, content, or services of these sites, phone numbers, companies, or products beyond the life of this book.

ISBN 978-1-4002-2387-9 (eBook)
ISBN 978-1-4002-2386-2 (HC)
ISBN 978-1-4002-2389-3 (SC)

Library of Congress Control Number: 2021934467

Printed in the United States of America
22 23 24 25 LSC 10 9 8 7 6 5 4 3 2 1

"After crosses and losses,
men grow humbler and wiser."

—Benjamin Franklin

CONTENTS

CONTENTS

PREFACE

ARE YOU LOOKING for a leadership book filled with academic concepts, eloquent and research-based notions, and lessons imparted by an intimidating and egocentric leader who knows exactly how to be successful because he's never failed?

If so, please keep looking. This book isn't for you.

I'm not the stereotypical CIA officer of the movies or books. I don't carry a leather-bound briefcase filled with high-tech spy gear, drive an exotic sports car, carry a gun around town, or stand six feet tall wearing a sharp blazer with a menacing expression on my face.

My voice is loud, and my laughter is even louder—being of Greek heritage, that's the only tone we have, and we embrace it fully. And I have a terrible tendency to interrupt, which drives my friends and family crazy. I'm working on fixing that, but it's a tough row to hoe for a type A personality. I'm that guy wearing a T-shirt and pair of jeans, driving in my Jeep Wrangler with thirty-five-inch tires and a lift kit, who volunteers to mow the lawn at the local high school baseball field where his son plays. I'm that guy who melts every time his little girl—now a fine, grown woman—calls to update him from college on how her day is going. The guy who excuses himself while on the phone with a journalist from the *Washington Post* because he has to go put the laundry into the dryer or do the dishes. Self-importance and ego are not part of my vocabulary.

If I had to choose a theme song to play in the background of my life, it wouldn't be the fast-paced, loud, and energetic tempo of the *Mission: Impossible* soundtrack. It would be a reassuring, comfortable, and familiar country song by Kenny Chesney that talks about pickup trucks, dirt roads, and the importance of family. You're not going to find me in a freshly pressed polo shirt at the golf course—I don't even play golf. Rather, I'm that guy in the RV at the Daytona 500 or sitting in the bleachers with my family at our beloved Washington Nationals baseball games. Don't waste your time looking for me at the most pretentious and overpriced restaurant in the nation's capital, because I'll be at my favorite dive bar in northern Virginia, the Vienna Inn, eating chicken wings and drinking beer with my buddies. A baseball hat with the Vienna Inn logo that I wore in Afghanistan for an entire year hangs on the wall. Go see for yourself; it's really there.

Yet I do have a refined side, which comes out at times. I have two degrees from Cornell University and have traveled the world twice over. I have briefed in the situation room at the White House, sat with kings and prime ministers, belong to a country club (mainly for the bar by the pool), have a twenty-year-old Rolex I can pull out on demand, and have attended more fancy diplomatic receptions than I care to remember. I'm an immigrant born outside this country and proudly worked for the CIA for twenty-six long years, before my body finally gave out and I had to retire.

So, what are you going to find in this book? I will present you nine leadership principles told through my personal stories at CIA, stories that I have never publicly revealed before and that will become your secret weapons to rise to the top of the ranks in whatever profession you are in.

So, welcome.

I promise you will enjoy the ride!

INTRODUCTION

THE TRUTH SHALL MAKE YOU FREE

I N HIGH SCHOOL travel baseball, parents lie and brag about their sons, coaches assuage the crazed parents to try and keep the peace, and social media is the epitome of wild exaggeration, where every young catcher has a 1.9 pop time and a fifteen-year-old pitcher throws a 90-mph fastball. But the players themselves know the truth—who really is solid both in the locker room and on the field, or who has a team-first attitude and who is only in it for themselves. At CIA, the same applies. We lie for a living, especially to foreigners. On the other hand, we must never lie to our colleagues, drawing a fine line of acceptable behavior. The truth, your integrity, is what sets you apart, as you so often operate on your own, with no supervision other than your conscience or your God or both. A clear mind, from practicing honesty, will allow you to sleep at night.

———

"AND YE SHALL know the truth and the truth shall make you free." This is the biblical verse, John 8:32, etched in the stone wall of the lobby at the Central Intelligence Agency headquarters at Langley, Virginia. It was former CIA director Allen Dulles, son of a minister, who wanted these words to become the motto of the CIA as they mirror the main core value of what the agency stands for: discover the truth and share it with the president, no matter what the implications would be for politics or political party. It is a professional ethos that "includes the core values of service, integrity, excellence, courage, teamwork, and stewardship" and that is talked about often and is deeply ingrained in every CIA officer from the very first steps they take into the CIA headquarters.[1]

These words are sacrosanct to me. I have lived by this ethos for twenty-six years—my entire career at CIA. My name is Marc Polymeropoulos. I was an operations officer by trade and one of CIA's most highly decorated field officers of my generation. I failed far more than I succeeded, and my ability to handle adversity was, ultimately, a key reason for my success. I am the recipient of the Distinguished Intelligence Medal, the Intelligence Medal of Merit, the Intelligence Commendation Medal, and the Distinguished Career Intelligence Medal. That's a lot of shiny hardware sitting on a shelf gathering dust in my basement, earned with blood and sweat from beating the pavement conducting tough street operations in some nasty places and against some truly fearsome adversaries.

My last position was overseeing all CIA clandestine operations in the Europe and Eurasia Mission Center. For the majority of my career, my specialty was working in the Middle East, both across the Levant and the Gulf, and also in the conflict zones of Iraq, Afghanistan, and North Africa. When I retired from the senior intelligence service ranks, my equivalent military grade was a four-star general. I have led thousands of the men and women of the CIA for the last two and a half decades in numerous clandestine operations and covert actions. Due to the very nature of my job, I have spent my life in the shadows. None of these operations were attributed to me or my teams at the agency, but the results of our work landed on the front pages of the *New York Times* and the *Washington Post,* and some were covered live by every media outlet on the planet. For this, and for many other reasons, I can say with great pride that I have had the unique experience of witnessing history—and often making history—from the center stage of the world. What an amazing journey my life and career have been. I am honored, fortunate, and indeed humbled to have been given the opportunity to serve with the men and women of the CIA, my home for twenty-six years.

The CIA

The Central Intelligence Agency is our nation's first line of defense. Like any other government agency, it was not built overnight. It went through several versions until, on July 26, 1947,

President Harry S. Truman signed the National Security Act, officially making the CIA what it is today. But before the CIA, there was the Organization of Strategic Services, also known as the OSS. Founded in 1942 and headed by the great general William Donovan, the OSS operated behind enemy lines during World War II and was also responsible for propaganda operations. Some of its most famous exploits included the insertion of "Jedburgh" teams, three-man units dropped into France in 1944 to help the resistance against Nazi occupation. The OSS was disbanded in 1945, after the United States dropped the atomic bombs on Japan. Many in the US government at the time, including Truman, thought such a spy organization was unsavory. But no president wants to be surprised in the middle of the night, so wisdom won the day. That original spirit of the OSS is still alive and can be seen with long-standing and oft-publicized CIA deployments to war zones such as Afghanistan and Iraq.

Today, the CIA has five "basic components, referred to as directorates. Each directorate plays a critical role in the intelligence cycle—the process of collecting, analyzing, and disseminating intelligence to top US government officials."[2] The basic mission of the CIA is simple and straightforward: collect and analyze foreign intelligence to assist the president and other policy makers in the US government in making national security decisions.

Most of the work performed at CIA is never seen by the general public, so it should come as no surprise that the work done by the Directorate of Science and Technology (DS&T) is highly classified. "The men and women—the scientists, engineers, and technical experts—in the DS&T produce technology so advanced, it's out of the science fiction genre. Think back to a James Bond movie and the work developed by the 'Q Branch.' What our men and women do is even more impressive. The use of science and technology is critical to the intelligence process, and the DS&T's mission is to attack intelligence problems with cutting-edge technical solutions to help protect the nation."[3]

The Directorate of Support (DS) "provides CIA personnel 24/7 with logistical support, medical services, security protection, and safe facilities—just to name a few of its mission-critical roles."[4]

Our operations officers from the Directorate of Operations (DO) collect the intelligence by recruiting foreigners—our agents—to provide nonpublic secret information about their countries, which is what I did for twenty-three of the twenty-six years of my career.

The Directorate of Digital Innovation (DDI) "is the agency's newest Directorate focused on accelerating innovation across the agency's mission activities with cutting-edge digital and cyber tradecraft and IT infrastructure."[5]

Our analysts (my original tribe for the first three of my twenty-six years at CIA) from the Directorate of Analysis (DA) then use human intelligence, along with other sources of collection such as imagery from satellites, signals intelligence from intercepted phone calls or coded messages, and open source information from the translation of foreign media, to formally assess what is happening on a given issue, and perhaps what will occur in the future. Such assessments are free of political bias and are provided in written or oral form to policy makers.

Finally, at times, the CIA is specifically and lawfully tasked by the White House to undertake covert action, which are activities that the CIA may take in other countries to accomplish a US foreign policy objective without the hand of the US government becoming known. This is the stuff of the CIA mystique, and some of it is quite controversial, such as (and this happened many decades ago) overthrowing Latin American governments and conducting seemingly bizarre mind-control experiments. Truth be told, those operations are far in the rearview mirror, and I had no experience with such activities. I was involved in multiple covert action programs, primarily in the counterterrorism arena. Some of these operations were the proudest events of my career and saved countless US lives. We worked hand in glove with the military—and in particular US special operations warriors who were some of the finest and bravest Americans I have ever met. One of my favorite quotes is attributed to George Orwell, who I believe quite succinctly summed up the work of the CIA and US military special operations teams fighting the war on terrorism. He stated, "People sleep peaceably in their beds at night only because rough men stand ready to do violence on their behalf." A glass paperweight with these words sits on my desk at home even today.

Diversity at CIA

Given the cultural fascination with the Central Intelligence Agency and people who work for it, I feel compelled to demystify stereotypical imagery and incorrect terminology associated with it. First of all, at CIA, we employ officers, not agents. Hollywood likes to call us CIA agents, but an agent is an individual—likely from a foreign country—whom we employ to spy for the United States. Intellect over brain and street smarts, real-world language ability and cultural acumen over fancy college degrees are some of our key traits. And blending into our surroundings is paramount. Our officers, me included, have different cultural, religious, and social backgrounds, and they often speak more than two languages as well. For example, I learned Arabic and Spanish at CIA and used my "kitchen" Greek when required.

The CIA has changed dramatically from the old 1950s caricature of being an Ivy League bastion of East Coast wealth and privilege. That is hardly the case in 2021. The CIA proudly states to new hires that we value diversity because we need diversity in order to be successful on the streets of the toughest arenas around the globe:

> The United States is one of the most diverse nations on earth. Our national heritage is built on the work, ideas, and beliefs of people from virtually every national origin, creed and culture. We achieve our greatest accomplishments when we draw on the talents of all parts of our society and bring diverse perspectives to our greatest challenges. Over the years, our Agency's successes—and even our failures—have taught us that an important key to carrying out our mission is to have diverse perspectives, cultural insights, language capabilities and skill sets to draw from when making decisions. Patriotism has no barriers; it is not based in gender, ethnicity, ability,

religion, or sexual orientation. CIA seeks patriots from every background and has made diversity and inclusion a key priority today and in the years to come.[6]

Finding the Operational Edge

One of the many reasons why I have always been proud of working at CIA is the value they place on diversity in its workforce—whether in gender, ethnic background, sexual orientation, or differently abled people. I saw the agency evolve over my twenty-six years, rather remarkably. Perhaps the events around September 11, 2001, were a significant catalyst, as not only did we hire more Arab Americans with critical Arabic languages skills, but those Arab Americans already in the organization were able to immediately shine and contribute in the ensuing war against al-Qaida.

I have a fond memory of a temporary duty assignment in East Africa, in 2002, where the station had three Arab American operations officers in the bullpen. One was of Iraqi origin, one with Egyptian heritage, and the other of Lebanese background. You would have thought that they would have gotten along famously, but they fought like brothers competing for scraps of food on the dinner table; it was hysterical. Different Arabic curses were exchanged, different dialects were used, and the rest of the bullpen watched in amused amazement. But they all were outstanding operators on the street, able to blend in both culturally and linguistically—a huge advantage for the US government in our efforts to rid the world of the scourge of al-Qaida—and two of them later rose to the top ranks of the CIA. I consider both to be friends, although they still would argue bitterly over any subject if we were having a beer at the Vienna Inn!

Female operations officers are also integral to the CIA. We cannot succeed without them. To me, as an operations manager in the Middle East, at times they were our secret weapon. Since in many Middle Eastern countries women still occupy a more traditional role, female operations officers were often more effective at handling our male Arab agents than were their male counterparts.

I recall reading an internal US government study of the family dynamics of the Arab world that highlighted the importance of the mother figure in the family, in particular in relationship to her son. I devoured this study and tried to put it into operation wherever I served in the Middle East. A successful female officer could exploit this dynamic by establishing a mother-son-like relationship with an agent. Once making clear that no physical or romantic relationship would ever happen between them, the female officer could establish herself as a motherly figure because an Arab male would often look for guidance from his mother in all aspects of his life, from his job to his marriage. Therefore, the female operations officer would become trustworthy and reliable to the Arab agent, a relationship we were able to maximize for full operational effect. From tasking our agents to steal classified documents from a safe in their foreign ministry or elicit secret information from their colleagues in their respective intelligence services, our female officers had that unique touch born out of the cultural dynamic of the Arab world. They became a sounding board for our agents' real fears in committing espionage, particularly if the sanction was prison or even death.

Female officers were able to fly under the radar since nobody in such male-dominated societies would suspect them of espionage. A female officer I knew well was getting ready to carry out an operational act, heading out to meet an agent on the streets of a country with a critical counterintelligence threat. In order to do so, she wore the hijab, a typical Arab headdress that women use in some Middle Eastern countries to partially cover their faces. We also had our female officers wear full burkas to operate without ever raising any suspicion. While our female officer was walking down the street, she felt as though she had crossed paths with somebody she recognized, but the encounter had been so brief that she couldn't quite put a name to the face. Still, something was off, and she had that sixth sense that she may have been recognized. Once back home after several hours on the street, she was not that surprised when her neighbor, whose grandfather was a senior aide to the country's president, approached her.

"Where have you been?" he asked in an accusatory tone.

It was him! she thought.

"I was just out shopping," she replied, her voice steady, slightly lifting the bag she was holding. "We needed some spices for the kibbe [an Arabic meatball of sorts] I will cook tonight."

His eyes lowered to look at the bag but quickly returned back to her, staring intently.

"Shopping, huh?" His right eyebrow raised. "Well, *sahtayn* [enjoy the meal]."

She smiled politely as he walked away.

Within several days, we received a report stating that this female officer was thought to be carrying out an operational act—that is, spying—which proved to the hostile local intelligence service that her husband must have been CIA. As the female officer and I read that report, we looked at each other in disbelief, then annoyance at the misogyny and chauvinism of the situation before laughing hysterically.

"Can you believe this?" she said. "Because I'm a woman, they don't think *I* could possibly be CIA! They are blaming only my husband!"

We made the easy call—shut her husband down operationally in-country but keep the female officer in the fight. Given that nobody suspected her because she was a woman, she continued to do her job, meeting our agents in this denied area (meaning a high counterintelligence threat) locale, proving once again that our female officers are invaluable to our clandestine missions and ultimately to our country's safety.

I recently told this story to a graduating class of newly minted operations officers, many of them female, to demonstrate the effectiveness of female operations officers in the Arab world. We win because of them.

Truth be told, the toughest, most accomplished, and most ethically sound leader I ever worked for was a female senior operations manager. She was responsible for saving thousands of American lives due to her role in the counterterrorism fight. She taught me the simple standard that I always tried to live up to, which was, "Do the right thing." I saw her stand up to numerous directors of the CIA, four-star generals, and White House officials. She remains one of my heroes to this day—but must remain unnamed. I admire that she doesn't care whether people know what she does for a living, but I hope that one day her story will be told. She is the single most important individual in the history of the US government's counterterrorism fight, an indispensable expert in her field. Yet this female officer would blend in at your local Walmart or Safeway as you both stand in line to pay for a gallon of milk, and that is exactly the way she wants it.

So, yes, diversity really matters, and the CIA wins because of it. As I retired, Gina Haspel had risen to serve as director of the CIA, a truly monumental achievement in a once male-dominated field. Similarly, the head of our Operations Directorate, Elizabeth Kimber, our nation's chief spy, was a gifted operations officer, empathetic, refined, and a brilliant linguist with an encyclopedic memory, who was tough as nails to our adversaries. I loved working for her, as she had complete faith in her officers, never micromanaged, and believed deeply in the importance of the organization. Two female officers at the apex of power in the intelligence community, a clear recognition of how far the agency and the country have come.

Becoming a CIA Officer

I entered on duty on January 3, 1993, as an analyst—having completed my master's degree, specializing in Algeria, from Cornell University—and spent two years working on South Asian and Middle East issues before transferring to the Directorate of Operations. Even though it is now much easier to go online and look for job openings at CIA, back in the early 1990s, recruiters visited college campuses looking for people interested in joining the agency. I knew from a very young age that I never wanted to have the classic nine-to-five job. I wanted more. More adventure, more fulfillment, more meaning, and I was a patriot and wanted to work for the US government. Isn't it interesting that so often those who come from another country (in my case, Greece) end up loving America and what it stands for so fiercely? That was me. I decided to speak with a recruiter, and that was how I began working at the only job I have ever had.

Looking back, I can't help but feel that every step I took since I was a child eventually led me to that conversation with the CIA recruiter. As an eighth-grader, I read James A. Michener's book *Caravans*, the story of a young foreign service officer in Afghanistan in the 1950s. I was mesmerized by this Lawrence of Arabia–type of tale, with its vivid description of Afghanistan, its tribes, and the concept of an American official serving far from home in a truly exotic land. One passage stands out to me the most, as I fully see myself in Michener's words: "I've been told that diplomats and military men remember with nostalgia the first alien lands in which they served, and I suppose this is inevitable; but in my case I look back upon Afghanistan with special affection because it was, in those days, the wildest, weirdest land on earth and to be a young man in Kabul was the essence of adventure."[7]

This adventure story ended up being oddly prophetic for me, as I spent considerable time in Afghanistan on several operational deployments years later. In March 2002, I was sitting cross-legged in a mud hut in southern Afghanistan across from an Afghan village elder, negotiating with him on building a well in exchange for the village's assistance in turning over a wanted Taliban commander we knew was in the area. The village elder betrayed us, and the Taliban had an ambush planned. If not for the smarts of our young Afghan interpreter, who was listening to chatter on the local radio net, I would not be here today. I recall calmly informing that village elder—and I am being diplomatic now compared to what I actually said—that if anything happened to us, the AC-130 gunship circling overhead would have something to say about it. If you had told me more than thirty-five years ago when I read Michener's book that I would be the one having such experiences one day in Afghanistan, I would not have believed you.

Long before Michener's book, my mind and view of the world had been shaped by my parents. My father, a not-so-religious Greek Orthodox, immigrated to the United States on a Fulbright scholarship to attend undergraduate school at Oregon State University and graduate school at Cornell University, and he then served as a college professor for almost four decades at Rutgers University. My mother was a Jewish girl from Long Island and the daughter of the treasurer of Temple Emanuel in Great Neck, Long Island, one of the biggest reform temples on the East Coast. Just like my father, she was a free thinker at Cornell. I would not be at CIA if not for adopting her practice of defying conventional wisdom and challenging myself to always seek out more. After all, she married a Greek and moved to Greece for a short time after finishing college, very much against the wishes of her shocked parents on Long Island.

Even back in the United States, my Greek heritage was quite important to my family, especially to my father, who would take me to Greek school on the weekends. I didn't like going there, and I would make my dislike known, so my father resorted to bribery. He took me to Dunkin' Donuts on the way there and McDonald's on the way back. He and I still laugh about it today. This routine went on for years, and it paid off, since I can still understand the language and am quite proud of my Greek heritage. We returned to the Greek islands for a month every summer through my college years. Mykonos, Greece, remains a magical place to me. Our household was always multicultural, and we celebrated both Greek and Jewish holidays—Passover, Easter, Christmas, Hanukkah, you name it. My grade school friends were jealous; I received more presents than anyone in class.

I was an only child and, after I was born in Greece, my parents settled down in Highland Park, New Jersey. I grew up a middle-class kid from a small college town, and I enjoyed listening to Bruce Springsteen and Jon Bon Jovi, hanging out with my friends on the Jersey shore, and sneaking into Rutgers fraternity parties. When I was ten years old, my parents divorced, and my father went to Algeria for a year to teach at a polytechnic university. One day, my mother—again defying conventional wisdom and the advice of my grandparents in Long Island—put me alone on an airplane to Algeria, with a stop in Paris, for a monthlong stay with my father. I can't even fathom doing that with my kids, but my mother was special. This trip made me fall in love with the Middle East, especially because my father, his best friend from Greece, and I traveled in a beat-up Volkswagen minibus more than two thousand miles through the Sahara, sleeping in a desert oasis, riding camels, and hiking sand dunes in a region that was not yet racked by an Islamic fundamentalist insurgency. It was the adventure of a lifetime. At my father's house in New Jersey, he still has a picture of me sitting on a camel from our incredible bonding trip to Algeria. My father later remarried, and he and my stepmother to this day travel the world, not missing a beat even in their eighties to experience new cultures and peoples.

Since both my parents had attended Cornell University, it was a no-brainer for me when it came time to choose a college. I was proud to be following in both my parents' footsteps, and I earned undergraduate and graduate degrees from Cornell, each year surviving the brutal winters of Ithaca, New York. While all my college friends went on to become lawyers or doctors or to work on Wall Street, I kept my eyes focused on the Central Intelligence Agency—I dare say, since I first slept in the desert oasis of Algeria.

Although I began as an analyst at the agency, I switched career paths after two years and became an operations officer. I remember how quickly my then supervisor and senior analyst, John Brennan, who went on to become CIA director from 2013 to 2017, agreed to my switch. I must not have been that great of an analyst to begin with!

Not long after that, I met an amazing woman—who also worked for the government and shared my desire for public service—who would eventually become my wife and the mother of our two children. My wife made me a better person from the beginning, challenging me with her intelligence, adventurous spirit, rock-solid ethics, and love of family. We now have a daughter and a son who are the joys of our lives, have grown up all over the world, and share our passion for adventure and learning.

My wife was born in Beirut, Lebanon, and was raised Catholic, so you can just imagine how vibrant our wedding was with all the Greek Orthodox, Jewish, and Catholic family members coming together for one big celebration, along with many Muslim friends from the Gulf and North Africa. My noble Jewish grandfather, who I thought would be horrified, actually welcomed this multicultural explosion and spoke beautifully at our wedding ceremony. It was a moment that our extended families have always cherished.

My Love for Baseball

My passion for CIA goes hand in hand with my love for baseball. I was six years old when my grandfather—my mother's father who gave the touching multicultural speech at my wedding—began taking me to games at Shea Stadium in Queens, New York, to watch the New York Mets. The Mets teams were consistently awful, which meant cheap tickets, but the memories of those times with my grandfather remain vivid to me to this day. Shea Stadium was famous for the planes from nearby LaGuardia Airport flying so low that players would call timeout during at bats. And during the early spring games, it got so windy in the cheap seats you felt like you would freeze to death. My grandfather would buy me everything from the ballpark, from souvenir bats and balls to bobbleheads of Mets players. We would go back to his house in Great Neck, Long Island—where my mom grew up—and have a catch or play Wiffle ball in his backyard. We didn't care how bad the Mets were; it was our time together and we reveled in both their struggles and in our loyalty—only true fans would follow such a terrible team. My grandfather played a special role for me in this respect, as my Greek father was not as well versed in the great American game of baseball.

Oddly enough, I became a Boston Red Sox fan later on in grade school, after my mother took me on several trips during the summers to Martha's Vineyard, Massachusetts, and I listened to Red Sox games on the radio from the village of Edgartown. I was hooked . . . and a Red Sox fan for life. Goodbye, NY Mets! I then suffered with the Red Sox for years, until they finally won their elusive World Series title in 2004, their first since 1918. This story of near epic suffering and historic failure appealed to me. Maybe that herculean struggle of the Red Sox, and even my earlier love of the lowly Mets, was a harbinger of my life in the CIA, where you need to learn so much about adversity before finding ultimate success. My son was two years old when the Red Sox won in 2004, but he claims to remember me jumping up and down and crying in our house in the Middle East as I watched my beloved Sox win it all on the Armed Forces Network.

Finally, in 2006, after my wife and I bought a house in northern Virginia and decided in 2011—after several overseas postings in the Middle East—that we would not move the family again, I have become a rabid Washington Nationals fan. Don't get me wrong, I still love the Red Sox, but we needed a local team and the Nationals fit the bill.

My son began playing baseball in the Middle East when he was eight years old, and he will continue playing in college next year. This is our bond, like the bond I had with my grandfather decades ago, and it has provided us incredible joy together. The Washington Nationals World Series title in 2019 was made even more special as my son and I attended four of the playoff games at Nats Park. I don't think I have ever screamed so loudly as I did at the wild card game against the Milwaukee Brewers on October 1, 2019. We were high-fiving each other, hugging strangers, screaming until we were hoarse, and I think I may have dumped a beer on my son's head after Juan Soto hit the go-ahead three-run single in the eighth inning! My baseball journey—from Shea Stadium in 1975 to Nats Park in 2019—is filled with a ton of failure, and an even greater measure of joy and redemption.

The Soul of the CIA

After twenty-six years of working at the CIA and spending every minute of my career in the shadows, never being able to disclose which operations I was working on or even where I was located—yet knowing very well what was going to appear worldwide on the front pages of newspapers because my officers and I had just made history happen—my friends have asked me why I am willing to finally speak out and even write a book about it.

It's an easy answer.

I want to share and give context to the American people about what I learned from working in an organization that I so deeply believe in. An organization that was not only my job but also my passion, my lifestyle, and my credo. The CIA has its own soul and culture, and there is so much good that we do. The CIA is also very much in the press these days, with a president who has publicly criticized the intelligence profession and has caused some significant angst in our ranks—and with me as well. Given this critical time in our nation's history, I feel compelled to translate to the outside world the leadership lessons I learned from this noble organization that remains an indispensable institution.

My recent retirement and the current journey I am enjoying in my new life of public speaking and writing has led me to engage in a great deal of introspection and soul searching on my career in the CIA. What did I enjoy most in my career? What will I miss most in retirement? In speaking with colleagues and reminiscing about our many decades at the agency, I kept coming back to a theme that is not always easy to put my finger on. It is simply the highly personal relationship—the closest feeling to love among a family—that many of us at CIA developed not just for the organization itself but mostly for each other as we served in the shadows without fanfare or distinction.

At times, we fought like cats and dogs, like a close-knit family. We complained about unfairness in promotions and job assignments, low pay, and bad cafeteria food. Nonetheless, we were a brotherhood and sisterhood that we would defend to the bitter end when attacked by outside forces.

I would always tell junior officers in their introductory meetings, the operations officer career is a calling and a lifestyle. It is not a nine-to-five or for the faint of heart, and it is done primarily at night and alone. It involves having immense intestinal fortitude and a willingness to engage in personal risk and sacrifice, with an ultimate belief that what we do in this gray and confused world is ultimately designed to protect those we love back in the United States and, just as importantly, to protect one another.

I used to start my talks with newly minted operations officers with the lines "There is no work-life balance. There is work. And there is how you can fit your life into work. My idea of a successful assignment for you is if you drag yourself up the ramp to the airplane when your tour is up."

Vignettes: My CIA Stories

My belief in the CIA and its people is best understood through a glimpse into several remarkable stories that exemplify some of what I love about this organization and its remarkable and committed workforce. My strong emotions for these heroes are not limited to the operations officer cadre. In fact, my kinship with my former colleagues in the analytic, support, and technical sides of the agency runs just as deep. Regardless of our role, we all contributed valiantly and in unique ways to the agency mission, and we supported each other through good times and rough ones, just like a family.

I have been asked many times, "Why do you do it? Why? With the long hours, the deployments away from your family, and the danger and death you must face?"

I've always responded the same. "We do it for each other."

These vignettes will provide you with a clearer explanation and background of my leadership philosophy. They go hand in hand with the Mad Minutes at the end of every chapter, so you can focus on the most important questions to ask yourself regarding your own leadership skills—something I have acquired and perfected while leading high-risk operations in high-stress environments, where failure can take on a whole new meaning, where success doesn't equal public acclaim or even recognition, and where, no matter what happens, the core value remains the unquestionable center of our being: "And ye shall know the truth and the truth shall make you free."

CLARITY
IN CRISIS

LEADERSHIP LESSONS FROM THE CIA

ONE

WHAT IS GREAT LEADERSHIP? CHARLIE'S WAY

'M SWEATING PROFUSELY in body armor, wearing night vision goggles. The helicopter is loud, and my thoughts are racing. I think of my family, who I know are so proud of me for volunteering for this assignment but are dreading that the unthinkable will happen to me. I think of Darren, another CIA officer I once led, who was in Afghanistan as well and killed here two years earlier, and his words to me when he left: he would make me proud. I never saw him again. I have been warned about indirect fire, unexploded mines, and insider threats. I'm flying into a remote location, where a group of American intelligence officers I have never met are waiting for my arrival. My task is brutally honest: lead a group of men and women in gathering intelligence against our foremost terrorist foes. We are the tip of the spear for the CIA in this never-ending fight against al-Qaida. I am our leader for the next year. I've done this before, years ago with Charlie, in Iraq. This is another frontline intelligence collection mission, so none of this is new. I got this—being in charge, the physical danger, the discipline needed to overcome fatigue, death, and failure. I am not a member of the US military; rather, I am a CIA officer trained in the art of human intelligence collection—recruiting and running spies who can operate comfortably in war zones. But a question still gnaws at me over and over as the helicopter is on its final approach to the landing zone: Am I really ready for this leadership challenge?

Twelve months later . . .

The helicopter lifts off, and my emotions are running wild. I am properly kitted out this time and look like I belong in these mountains. The bushy beard, the longer hair. So different from a year ago. There are tears in my eyes. I just said farewell to both the American CIA heroes that I led and our local allies whose bravery I admired. I honestly believe they will miss me, that I put it all on the line, and that they know how much I cared for them. I worry that any one of them will get hurt in the near future. We accomplished a great deal in the year, and our enemy is far weaker and less of a threat to the United States than when we arrived. I think of my family, how I made them proud, and how now is the time for me to return home to be a husband and a father. Finally, I recall that initial flight a year prior, when I had asked myself how I would lead such a group of intelligence warriors and if I were ready for such a challenge. I smile and nod. I never stopped learning, and I know it will take many months for the leadership lessons to sink in. I take heart from a colleague of mine, a far more accomplished leader than I, a legend in the paramilitary ranks, who told me upon my departure, "When it's all said and done, you did it right." I also know that Charlie would have been proud. He would have had a glass of bourbon in one hand, a cigar in another, and would have given me a big bear hug.

WHAT IS GREAT LEADERSHIP? I asked myself this very question many times as a young CIA operations officer, so much so that it became a goal of mine to find the right answer.

First and foremost, I think of a mentor of mine, a senior officer we will call Charlie. He was always hesitant to accept individual awards as he believed only the group that he led was worthy of such praise. He relished the successes of his subordinates, gave praise to others for heroic actions he accomplished, opened his home to officers who were under his command, and always had a smile on his face. From kings, prime ministers, and the heads of foreign liaison services, to the everyday street sweeper in the back alleys, Charlie was known just by his first name throughout the Middle East. From the day I walked into the headquarters building, he has had the greatest impact on my career not only in terms of what he taught me about the art of espionage but also about caring for the people under his command.

My most important memory of Charlie, which I have never told anyone publicly before, is from late summer 2003 after we had returned from Iraq. I was not in a good mental state. My wife feared (correctly) that I was suffering from some form of PTSD due to recurring nightmares of dead, charred, dismembered bodies that would jar me awake at night and the anger that would cause me to lash out during the day at the most mundane issues, such as the mail being late or the garbage truck missing a pickup. After the intensity of being on the ground during the initial fight for Baghdad, running agents while working closely with naval special warfare units, I was not well. Professional help was in order, but Charlie first suggested that our team have a reunion on Cape Cod, the location of his beloved summer cottage. All of us, husbands, wives, and children included, spent two weeks decompressing on the beach over lobsters and barbecues. It was a magical time for me and my family that ultimately helped in my healing. I needed to feel safe, to find time to talk about what I experienced. Amazingly enough, it worked, as my nightmares subsided. Charlie understood that we were still in need of being together as a team, even back in the United States.

Great leaders promote family values.

When Charlie recently and suddenly passed away, the outpouring of love and emotion at his funeral spanned generations of CIA officers as well as many in the Arab world he had come in contact with. He was a true icon of leadership at CIA. I will never forget him.

Unfortunately, not all our senior officers were as outstanding as Charlie. Some officers constantly berated their subordinates, ruling through fear and intimidation. I remember an officer openly cursing at me during a meeting with the White House, after which close friends at work had to talk me off the ledge from quitting when I returned to my desk at the CIA headquarters in Langley, Virginia. Other senior officers had unpredictable cruel streaks that would bite all of us without warning. I'm pleased to note that most of these types were slowly but surely drummed out of the CIA, as their time had certainly passed.

Even though the knowledge I acquired while working with both outstanding senior officers and those who were just plain dreadful equipped me with a clear view of what type of leader I wanted to become one day, it did not provide me with a complete answer to my main question: What is great leadership?

Over time, my many experiences in the dark and dangerous streets of the third world countries did provide me an answer. My career in the CIA was a thrilling one filled with lots of ups and downs, but still one that made me feel accomplished and proud of the role I played not just in the agency but also in the world. From running an agent who caught spies betraying the United States, to flying into Baghdad with naval special warfare units in 2003 and leading the hunt for Iraqi regime high-value targets (HVTs) using an operational network I had helped to develop, to helping the CIA hunt down and neutralize the leadership of al-Qaida across the globe, to eventually overseeing operations for the CIA across Europe and Eurasia during Russian attempts to subvert our democracy— I had a front-row view of many major world events over the last three decades. As I would always tell my junior officers, it was not difficult to get up each morning regardless of where I was in the world. I was fired up to come to work every day in my career. "Game on," I would say to myself each morning as I walked into one of our overseas facilities or at our headquarters, passing by the famed CIA Memorial Wall, with stars etched into the white Alabama marble signifying the 133 CIA officers killed in the line of duty.

The Officer and the Agent

As noted in the introduction, the primary role of an operations officer is to spot, assess, develop, recruit, and run agents. Considering the combination of secrecy, unpredictability, and danger inherent in the work, what pushes someone to become an agent? What motivates an individual to decide to commit espionage against his or her country? Historically, people who have taken such a step have done so for several reasons: from purely ideological ones—during the Cold War, for example, the global struggle between communism and capitalism—to financial reasons. Perhaps it is out of desperation for money they need to give their children a better education or to cover health-care costs for a sick relative. And sometimes it boils down to narcissism and a desire to get revenge against colleagues or systems that they feel have wronged them, such as a glass ceiling in their country that prevents them because of their minority status from getting a promotion. I would also add that, in the case of war zone operations, a primal motivator has been to jump on board the side with the greatest firepower at the time, which was the position the US occupied during its invasions of Iraq and Afghanistan. The role of a US intelligence officer is to identify such vulnerabilities and what might be motivating a target, and then over time exploit them to convince the individual to provide the United States with secret information. It comes down to the most basic type of human interpersonal relationships. I liked to call it a romance, and then a marriage.

Charlie was the first senior CIA officer to truly teach me about the art of recruiting and handling agents. His skill in making an agent feel that they were the most important person on the planet was legendary. Don't be patronizing, yet don't be a pushover. Treat the agent with respect, yet be firm and make sure you are in control. Get to know your agent and his or her family. Charlie was the flat-out best operations officer I have ever encountered.

A recruitment is an incredibly intimate relationship. In the end, you are looking at someone who says, "I am putting my life in your hands." Now let me be clear: we, meaning the US government, give them a great deal in return, whether it be finances or some other reward. But in the end, the responsibility that a young operations officer has in a relationship with a recruited agent is like no other job in the US government.

I was introduced to one of my favorite agents of my career when I was sent to another country to train this agent on secret communications systems. He proved amazingly resilient and upbeat during the training sessions. During his time on the streets, he proved highly disciplined at sending in reports, providing us a unique view on the inner workings of his country's rotten government. Our agent loved the American way of life and the political and economic freedoms that America stood for. This is what drove him, as he felt that one day his country's leadership would fall and that he would help usher in a new era in which the American ideal could prosper. I never met him for long on the streets of his country, as even brief meetings were considered dangerous, yet he never missed our monthly meeting in more than two years of internal handling. Not one. During a meeting out of country, in which we were able to speak and interact more freely, he provided me with words that I have remembered to this day.

"Marc, never forget, my life and the life of my family is in your hands. You may forget me day to day as you are busy with your life, as you go to a restaurant at night with your wife, watch a soccer match on TV, or enjoy time with your family on the weekends, and then you return home to the United States for the month during the summer."

He then looked at me so intently, it felt as if he were staring into my soul. There was a long silence between us. "But make no mistake, I think of you, actually *you* personally, each and every day. If you make one single mistake in our meeting and communication arrangements, I may die. And my family will suffer as well. You have to be perfect, and I need to always assure myself that this is the case, so I think of you all the time."

His words shook me for days. The weight of the world had been placed upon me. His speech fueled my desire to keep him productive and alive, employing the highest traditions of the CIA. When our agent ultimately elected to leave his country for a new life, I finally breathed easier as I knew he and his family would never be harmed. He was a hero to his country, to the United States, and to me. Pretty heavy stuff for a young operations officer. I'm not sure that those in the media who, at times, denounce the CIA actually understand what we do and the responsibilities we have, both in collecting critical information from our agents and, just as important, keeping them alive. It's a deeply personal business. The stories of every agent I ever recruited and handled, most whom I met on dark street corners or conducted brush passes with in dusty alleyways, are forever seared into my memory.

Great Leadership

After almost three decades of working at CIA, first learning from legends such as Charlie and then gaining experience as I moved throughout the Middle East, I finally have a good idea of what it takes to lead in high-stress environments and what failure can *really* mean. Over time and a great deal of trial and error—some of it unfortunately involving the loss of human life—I refined my own leadership philosophy. A leadership philosophy that is as applicable to other lines of work as it was successful in the intelligence world.

Imagine you're a football player on a team preparing for the biggest season of your career. Or you're on an emergency room team made up of doctors, nurses, and administrative staff, working in a high-crime area with dim hope for relief over the next six months. Or you're a junior sales executive who wants to advance in your career and sees a promotion around the corner, but you're not clear on what it will take to lead a team and practice great leadership. My principles will help people in all these circumstances and in all walks of life. When you come right down to it, leadership is about inspiring and getting the best from others—and no matter what line of business we're in, we are all in the People Business. This transcends every field and every technical specialty, and the lessons I've learned from leading my fellow officers and field staff are directly translatable to every leadership scenario, including yours, and they can be applied to groups as small as two and as big as two thousand.

So, what is great leadership?

Great leadership is the art of willing those around you to conduct activities that are:

- Righteous—legal, ethical, and moral. Great leaders cannot ask their subordinates to break the law or commit a crime. The tasks must have a higher purpose and be within the bounds of our legal and moral compass.
- Difficult—the task at hand is not your everyday chore. It is a task that may entail sacrifice, risk, both physical and emotional, and something out of your comfort zone.
- Selfless—many in your group would never choose to tackle the task on their own, and you must never ask others to do what you would not.
- Communicable—the task must be easy to explain within the group, and you must accept honest feedback, both positive and negative.

I call my leadership philosophy Clarity in Crisis. In this book, I will share nine core principles for outstanding leadership, provide real-world examples of how I employed them during my career as an operations officer for the CIA, and show you how to meet any crisis head-on and lead through it. These core concepts are:

1. The Glue Guy
2. Adversity Is the Performance-Enhancing Drug (PED) to Success
3. The Process Monkey

4. Humility Is Best Served Warm
5. Win an Oscar
6. Family Values
7. Be a People Developer
8. Employ the Dagger
9. Finding Clarity in the Shadows

Each principle builds on the next and is designed for real-world applicability when you need it most, operating under time constraints and with less than ideal situational awareness, or smack dab in the middle of a crisis. It is user friendly to the core. You will learn to embrace ambiguity with no fear, so that when the moment arises, leadership will come naturally to you in any situation. From a street fight in Afghanistan to a boardroom meeting in New York City, these concepts are universal. In addition, after each core concept—which will be explained through the use of personal stories, vignettes, and which will highlight ways to put them into practice—I will also give you a checklist, which at CIA is what we call the Mad Minute. We use this checklist when planning operational meetings and key tasks that an operations officer is required to cover immediately with their agents. You can use these Mad Minutes and apply my principles to your own life and career, regardless of your profession.

There is no secret sauce here, just tried-and-true leadership principles that I honed while serving in some of the wildest places on the planet.

Are you ready to learn how to be a great leader?

TWO

THE GLUE GUY

DAVID ROSS PLAYED for fourteen years in the major leagues with seven teams, winning two World Series titles with the Red Sox and the Cubs. He was a catcher (my son's position, so I'm predisposed to these guys) and learned a thing or two about leadership and what constitutes a championship-level team. In 2017, Ross summed up the concept of the Glue Guy as follows: "It's a guy who's unselfish and who's a good teammate. A guy who communicates well and who's honest with his teammates and himself. Somebody the other guys can count on to offer advice or encouragement. He keeps everybody loose but, at the same time, focused. Basically, it's a guy who—in baseball clubhouses that often have age gaps, varying talent levels, and even language barriers—just sort of keeps everything together."[1]

Ross gave a great snapshot of the Glue Guy in the professional baseball world. And here's what it means in high school baseball: when your assistant coach gives you the hit-and-run sign and a runner is on the move from first base, your only responsibility is to swing the bat. If the pitch is a high fastball, you better execute a tomahawk chop, swing at a terrible pitch, even if your teammates will mock you mercilessly in the dugout.

At CIA, the principle of the Glue Guy is alive and well, albeit with a twist. It is executing a simple task—such as procuring a safe house smartly and securely; the first step in a series of events that leads to a successful operation. It is providing countersurveillance to a colleague who is meeting an agent with secret information that could change US policy. These support roles are just as important as the home run or the takedown of an HVT, because neither will happen if the Glue Guy or Gal doesn't set it up.

———

AS A CIA officer, I traveled and moved often, but I was also able to bring my family along with me most of the time—when I wasn't going to a war-torn country—which made my children's childhoods that much more fun as we visited Petra in Jordan, Palmyra in Syria, and the Great Pyramids of Giza in Egypt. While in one Arab country, my son—who at the time was only eight years old—became interested in baseball. So I had him join a coed team, which my daughter, two years his senior, was able to take part in as well. The field was made of dirt, not grass. I succeeded at containing any thoughts about the oddities between the baseball I knew in America and the baseball I was seeing here . . . until the local coach threw a pitch underhanded.

"Hey!" I yelled, jumping out of the stands and marching across the field. I could feel the stares of people in attendance. "That's not how you do it!"

The coach looked at me in shock, eyes wide open. Who was this crazy American?

"You threw underhanded!" I screamed as I grabbed the ball from his hand. "You can't teach these kids baseball by throwing underhanded. You're fired!" My friends from the office were laughing uncontrollably, their cell phones out to record the absurd situation.

And that's how I became my son's first baseball coach, a role I took seriously, especially when he returned to the US and started playing catcher two years later in an organized Little League.

I'll never forget when my wife asked him how he was enjoying Little League and he said, "It was okay, Mom. The only thing was that there was grass all over the field; it was so weird." My wife had to then explain that it was customary for a baseball field to be mostly grass, unlike the dusty dirt fields of the Middle East where he first picked up a bat!

I'll also never forget what his first two seasons of Little League were like. He was way behind the talent level of other players who had been on the ball field for years playing on organized teams. You know what it's like to see other parents and players wince when your son comes up to bat because they know an out is coming? That was him. It was hard for a loving parent to watch. So that winter we practiced together each night, religiously, when I came home from work. It didn't matter if I was tired or he had more homework to do; we would go to a local baseball training academy and he would either hit, throw, run sprints, or learn the finer points of catching. I remember one time I looked at his batting gloves and saw blood seeping through from blisters, but he never complained. He would say, "Let's keep going."

"Damn, that sounds like me at work," I thought.

I was proud to witness his transformation. He began to fully embrace a herculean work ethic, and all his blood and sweat paid off the very next season when he hit eighteen home runs and became a Little League all-star. He earned every accolade he received, and I was so proud of him given the strides he had made over the previous winter. Eventually, this fierce work ethic and dedication led him to play on a famed, nationally ranked East Coast travel team, and he was a four-year varsity letter winner in high school and captain of his team his senior year. But he also evolved as a leader. He's five foot seven and 180 pounds, not an ideal size for a serious college or pro prospect. So he was not recruited by Division I colleges but by Division III colleges. He was not written about by national scouting services, but rather by our local hometown newspaper. He was elite—but not the star on the teams he played on. My son does plan to play in college, which will be the culmination of an extraordinary journey that began on the dirt baseball fields of the Middle East. And he has turned into exactly who he strove to be—a very good baseball player and an elite Glue Guy.

In baseball, as in any other sport, it is critical to have players who are willing to sacrifice, don't complain, and make others better. When putting together a championship team, these players are just as important as the most valuable player because they are the ones who hold the team together—the Glue Guys—or Gals.

The Glue Guy is my favorite leadership principle, and I followed it faithfully in every management job that I served in at CIA. Like every organization, we employed people with a variety of skill sets. We had our operations officers, who were our "tip of the spear," running and recruiting foreign agents to spy for the United States. That was me. There were analysts, incredibly well educated with multiple languages and a steely determination to tell the truth to sometimes skeptical policy makers. Then, there were our support officers, who could procure a vehicle in a third world country in hours, fix a broken septic system in the middle of the African jungle, or find tickets to the ballet for you and a developmental target. At each of the stations I managed, I valued our support staff—the Glue Guys—as much as anyone else. I did not want a homogenous team of all-stars with too many egos involved, each rushing for individual glory.

A successful intelligence operation is predicated upon precisely the same concept, where everyone has a job to do and each one is as important as the last. In an operation to take down an HVT in Iraq, for example, there were multiple pieces that constituted a raid in Iraq. After the invasion of Iraq in 2003, we had tracked a target—one in the Deck of Cards, the fifty-five most wanted Iraqi regime officials—and he was in our sights. The surveillance team spent weeks on target, patiently gathering pattern of life—where a target goes to work, lives, goes shopping, etc.—on the HVT. The assault team from the US military planned to grab the HVT at a defined location that was free from hostile forces. And the penetration agent—the spy—that we'd recruited from within the regime and who was being handled by one of our operations officers (me) was going to give us the final signal letting us know that the HVT was in place for capture. Meanwhile, the unsung support officer in the rear had procured disguise kits and printed out the most recent satellite imagery for use by the CIA team members on the ground. So who was the most important officer in this operation? Was it the lead member of the assault force, who received the glory from the headlines? Was it me, who handled the agent that led us to the HVT? I would argue that it was the support officer, the Glue Guy.

Every successful team has such men and women, and as a leader, your job is to search out these indispensable, behind-the-scenes employees. Looking back, I should have shared the Distinguished Intelligence Medal—which I received from my time in Iraq—with our support officers; they deserved it as much as I did.

How to Spot the Glue Guy or Gal

The Glue Guy can be found in every team, company, and organization. In an emergency room team that includes doctors, nurses, and administrative staff, I would suggest that the nurses are the Glue Guys and Gals. Even though they are not the ones operating on the patients, they are the ones who stand behind the scenes and make sure the entire operation is running smoothly, helping doctors—the ones in the spotlight—achieve their goals safely and eventually leading the whole team to success. My stepbrother, Matt, runs an emergency room in the New York City area; he is a top dog of his profession, providing frontline trauma care, treating everything from gunshot wounds to victims of barroom brawls to the everyday flu. He has been heroic on the front lines of the COVID-19 epidemic. Yet he openly states that the nurses are the rock of the hospital—and a critical cog of the machine that is the chaotic emergency room in America's busiest city.

Take it from the emergency room to the football field. I once gave a speech to a high school football team in my hometown of Vienna, Virginia, where I addressed this very topic. I asked Ry, our resident stud six-foot-five quarterback, who was heading off to play Division I football at William and Mary, "Who is your Glue Guy?" Ry had a tremendous senior season and helped carry the team to a winning record. Yet he responded with no hesitation that it was his entire offensive line. The table of offensive linemen started high-fiving each other and cheering wildly. What a great response! Ry gets it.

So how can you identify your Glue Guy or Glue Gal? What are the personality traits a person must possess in order to be relied upon so much that they become the glue that holds the team together?

First and foremost, the Glue Guy needs to be selfless and have a team-first attitude. He or she is not looking for the glory or for the accolades. At the same time, it is important that you—the leader—motivate and celebrate your Glue Guys. Openly recognize and praise the Glue Guys for the hard work they put into keeping the team together and, ultimately, making the entire operation a success.

As the CIA leader in a field station or base, during my morning meetings, I would always include not only our operation officers but also the support and finance officers, because they were integral to the success of our operations. When we had an agent whom we didn't completely trust, we would often put a countersurveillance team on the street who would watch the operational site where the officer was going to meet the agent. They would be looking for people who shouldn't be there, such as the host nation's security personnel or individuals from a terrorist group who might be trying to set up an ambush.

How did we find officers for this role? More often than not, they were highly motivated volunteers from the station who wanted to help out and who told management about it. These fellow operations officers or individuals from other job categories possessed the requisite training, which is even more astonishing considering what a thankless job this was—standing on the street corners for hours on end. They were not the actual operations officers meeting the agent who would get all the accolades for obtaining the vital intelligence. No, they were the ones who, while conducting countersurveillance, might observe anomalies indicating that there was danger ahead. They then had the enormous, yet unheralded, responsibility to signal the operations officer to abort the meeting.

One time in the Middle East, I was en route to an operational meeting with an untested contact whose country was a bitter enemy of the United States, which made the meeting even more dangerous. I recognized one of our countersurveillance officers loitering in an alleyway. He had been in the area for hours, moving spots so as not to "heat up" his location and get caught but always with the goal of being in position to protect me when my meeting went down. When the operation was over late that night, we gathered in a neighborhood bar and I toasted him with gusto for his behind-the-scenes efforts. He shrugged off my repeated offers to buy a round of drinks, simply noting that his job was part of the "brotherhood of our profession."

"Brother," he added, "that was better than sitting behind a desk any day. Plus, you looked ridiculous in your disguise, and the body armor you were wearing made you look like a Weeble."

Glue Guys do unsung acts for the team without batting an eye. And my partner that day? He has risen high up in our organization. Yet every time I have seen him since that operation nearly twenty years ago, I've made sure to thank him again for his willingness to be the Glue Guy. I'll keep trying to get him to come to the Vienna Inn. Round's on me, of course.

Glue Guys at CIA were not just ordinary support personnel. At times, they were the real unheralded MVPs. Think of Charlie O'Brien, the solid defensive catcher who all-star caliber pitchers would line up to try and play with. Think of the clubhouse attendants of the 2019 World Series–winning Washington Nationals. The players thought so much of them that they rewarded them with World Series rings and bonuses of $10,000 or higher. It was their way of saying thank you to the support personnel who did the laundry, prepared the locker room, and performed the grunt work, ultimately ensuring that the players were taken care of.

Our Docs

When I think about true Glue Guys, I think about the physician assistant (PA) on CIA deployments to war zones such as Iraq and Afghanistan, as some of the most critical members of the team. I loved these officers. At times, we may have been days away from formal medical care, so our PAs—whom we affectionately call "Docs"—were the first line of trauma care. From treating the innumerable and grotesque gastrointestinal illnesses that I was unfortunately famous for contracting and that could literally shut down a base—denying our ability to send officers to meet agents, for example, because everyone was so sick—to performing lifesaving care for both our officers or indigenous personnel, we simply could not operate without our PAs.

Yet they did all of this behind the scenes, with little fanfare, and always with positive attitudes. When we needed our PAs, we really needed them. But after an officer obtains critical intelligence from an agent about the location of an HVT, do you think the PA is always lauded? Of course not, and I certainly made my share of mistakes in not offering such praise. But the operations officer could not have gone outside the wire had the PA not been on-site, ready to respond if required.

In Afghanistan, at our austere base, decades of war had made the mountainous region where we were stationed incredibly dangerous due to thousands of land mines that the then Soviet Union had dropped even in civilian areas.

One day, a junior officer came running into the gym where I was going through my morning workout, which I held dear to me for stress relief and did not like it interrupted. He was panting and trying to catch his breath.

"Young boy . . . probably ten . . . stepped on a land mine!" He turned around and we both ran toward the gates of the base.

What I saw at the makeshift triage area stopped me in my tracks. The boy was lying on a stretcher in a pool of his own blood.

"Critical condition, call in the Nine Line," one of the base officers calmly stated. The Nine Line is typically a medical evacuation request for a soldier injured on the battlefield. In this case, it was a young boy.

"Ten years old," stated another trained professional in a clear, crisp tone.

I heard somebody else yell, but all the voices now seemed to be coming from a completely different world, echoing from far away.

My daughter is ten years old.

My chest hurt. I placed a hand over my heart. Within a matter of seconds after I arrived at the scene, our PA—plus another base officer who was a former ER nurse in Baltimore and a former special forces medic as well—offered frontline trauma care to the ten-year-old boy who was dying right before our eyes. He was screaming as we brought him on base, his parents in a panic, and only minutes to spare in order to save his life. I kept looking at his father, who seemed terribly helpless. I could not even begin to imagine what they were going through at that moment, but I sure knew that their child was in great hands in the care of our amazing PA and other base personnel.

The way my CIA team responded to save this child was inspirational. That day, I saw something special. As our PA and others worked to stabilize the child, the US Army Blackhawk helicopter arrived to evacuate him to a US military hospital. I will never forget watching in awe as our blood-soaked personnel, led by our PA, frantically worked on him and then placed him on the waiting helicopter.

After receiving confirmation that the boy's life was no longer in danger after surgery and that he would make it through this horrifying experience, I addressed the team that night in an impromptu all-hands meeting.

"I just want to say," I began, choking a bit on my own words, "you all just got it done today. You got it *done*. That was . . ." My voice trailed off as pictures of my ten-year-old daughter flashed before my eyes. "You did some hero work; you saved that boy's life, no doubt." There was quiet, as the other base personnel were similarly moved by what had occurred. These were a bunch of tough warriors, but they knew that these circumstances were unique and something we could all relate to, as so many of us had kids at home. I had just witnessed one of the singularly proudest moments I have ever encountered at CIA.

One of my officers, seeing me struggling, put his arm around me and said, "Hey, boss, pretty beast move by the Doc. That was some badass hero shit."

"Right on," I thought, smiling.

It was as simple as that. The CIA "Docs"—our PAs—are the classic Glue Guys.

The Frozen Pig

Prepackaged Meals Ready to Eat (MREs), and US military mess hall food, with its thousands of calories guaranteed to stop you up—if you have ever served in a war zone, these delicacies have a special place in your heart, and in your stomach. At the CIA, we have managed to employ fantastic cooks—whom I called by the simple moniker "Chef"—at our frontline bases. The agency has fully grasped the notion that a well-fed intelligence officer is both happy and healthy and, most importantly, exponentially more productive.

The food at CIA bases in the years since September 11, 2001, has become something of a legend across the entire intelligence and special operations communities for the amazing quality. Everyone from generals to the operators would always try and drop in and sneak a meal with us because we just did it right. I learned quickly how important it was to get to know our chefs during my numerous deployments to war zones. I made a point to both thank them simply for their outstanding culinary skills under difficult conditions—and even under indirect fire attacks in some locations—but even more so, to have them understand that they were critical parts of the team. In fact, at one location, during my weekly "all hands"—which was designed for the intelligence personnel with appropriate clearance levels and was where we would discuss the week's operational developments and plan for the days ahead—I would skirt the rules a bit and invite our chef for the beginning or end of the session. I wanted him, particularly when we celebrated a success, to understand that he was a key component of our team.

Some of my favorite moments with our chefs were at the holidays, when our officers would often suffer in silence, terribly missing their families. I actually embraced these times, as I felt that, as a leader, I could make a difference in showing that I truly cared. Chef was integral to this key morale-boosting time, and I'll never forget being at a drop zone (DZ), waiting for a C-17 to deliver us key supplies via parachute, which on this particular occasion—and per my very carefully concealed request—included a full-on frozen pig. I went to the DZ that day to ensure the pig was in the food supply drop, and it sure was, frozen white and rock-solid. The looks on the faces of our officers later that week were priceless. We had an incredible holiday dinner, courtesy of our remarkable chef. What a classic example of the Glue Guy.

Conclusion

It is important, for the success of your own company, organization, and workplace, that you as the leader of your team recognize your Glue Guys and Gals. Be sure to validate their efforts and reassure them that, even though they work in the shadows, you and the rest of the team see them, appreciate them, and value them. And to all my readers who have identified themselves as the Glue Guys and Gals of their own workplaces, I'd like to shake your hand and virtually invite you to join me at the Vienna Inn for a couple of frosty ones and some chicken wings, spicy, extra crispy, with double blue cheese dressing on the side!

THE GLUE GUY MAD MINUTE

- Identify by name and/or job title your Glue Guys or Gals and think about why they are so key to your success.
- Give an example of a Glue Guy success story in your work unit.
- Ensure they are not ignored during planning sessions, as they are the foundations for your success.
- Ensure they are celebrated after successes, just as much as your "tip of the spear" personnel.

THREE

ADVERSITY IS THE PERFORMANCE-ENHANCING DRUG TO SUCCESS

"MARC POLYMEROPOULOS IS hereby awarded the Distinguished Intelligence Medal in recognition of this exceptional performance during Operation Iraqi Freedom. During this challenging assignment, Mr. Polymeropoulos exhibited unwavering dedication to mission success, superior organizational skills and a remarkable talent for anticipating contingencies. He also has an innate ability to forge cooperative and productive relationships with other officers as well as external organizations such as the US Military and foreign government officials. He possesses inspirational leadership, innovative operational creativity, and tenacity and focus that enabled an unqualified success for this Agency's contribution to Operation Iraqi Freedom. Mr. Polymeropoulos' tireless efforts and commitment to professional excellence are in keeping with the highest traditions of our service and reflect great credit on him, the Central Intelligence Agency, and the Federal service."

———

AS I'VE PREVIOUSLY mentioned, I was one of the most highly decorated CIA officers of my generation. I have humbly achieved great successes in my career, which I am incredibly proud of, especially because of what they meant in terms of keeping our country safe. But do you really want to know how I was able to become that successful, to the point of earning the Distinguished Intelligence Medal?

I failed.

Not just once.

Often.

And in droves.

But I came to terms with my failures.

I'd like to make one thing clear: I've been on the front line in Afghanistan and Iraq. I know what I'm talking about when it comes to extreme pressure and mortal danger. There is no *real* sanction for failure on the baseball diamond, unlike what the men and women from CIA face, along with our colleagues in the US military. Yet the complementary lessons one can take from both a simple game involving a ball, bat, and glove, and the basic espionage profession involving the recruitment of human agents, are actually quite profound.

In baseball and recruiting operations, failing seven times out of ten are excellent odds. If I attended an event—for example, a diplomatic reception at the Syrian embassy in another Middle Eastern capital—where I was hoping to meet a potential recruitment target, and that night I wasn't successful, I would try again the next night. And the next night. And—you guessed it—the next night. But what I wouldn't do was give up on trying to recruit the agent I knew we needed in order to fill a critical intelligence gap. Hitting a baseball is very hard. Gaining foreign adversaries' trust so that they betray their country for the benefit of ours is also highly complex and difficult. If you succeed, you make an all-star team or receive a promotion. Hitting .300 will keep you on the top of both professions. That is the magic number. But the key to achieving that magic number is coming to terms with the reality that you must experience and understand failure.

Espionage operations always strive to do the seemingly impossible, such as finding answers to tough and complex questions: What is Vladimir Putin planning in terms of interfering with the 2020 elections? Are the North Koreans going to keep testing their nuclear weapons?

On the other hand, so is hitting a curveball, which seems to defy physics, dropping as if it has a twenty-pound weight attached to it, making it nearly impossible to make contact. Whether holding a bat or an intelligence briefing, both demonstrate how success is hard to come by. Life can be inherently unfair, so it is how you respond to such adversity that will ultimately make you a better player or a better intelligence officer. There is a mental game played in both fields, so much so that one defeats one's adversary not only on the basis of talent but on work ethic and the ability to compartmentalize the repeated bouts of failure that bring lesser men and women to their knees.

In baseball, you learn to fail and suffer. If you can't handle the failure, you can't succeed in the game. At some level, you stop being the best and, for you to maintain even the ability to stay in the lineup, you must work your tail off. In recruitment operations, or when hunting HVTs in Iraq or Afghanistan, the same applies. You will fail, but you cannot give up, because no one else is standing on the ramparts guarding America. Failing is an option. But overall failure—quitting, not pulling up your bootstraps for the next night—is not. The key is never to give up and throw in the towel. Adversity builds solid ballplayers and intelligence officers alike, individuals who are so mentally tough that they can brush off the negative and tackle the next challenge without any peripheral noise in their head. I once knew an officer who, after something went astray, used to say to himself, "Wow, that was hard to stomach. Let me really think about how I feel, and what I did, because I don't want to go through this again." That officer was, of course, me.

Simply put, you need to feel what it is like to be at rock bottom before you're able to find success.

Think of the Boston Red Sox's epic seven-game victory over the New York Yankees in the 2004 American League Championship Series, after losing to them in heartbreaking fashion the year before. In 2003, Aaron Boone of the Yankees hit a walk-off home run to send the Red Sox home. The next year, after being down 3-0 in the series, the Red Sox staged one of the most miraculous comebacks in sports history, winning four straight games. Therefore, 2004 does not happen had the brutality of 2003 not been experienced, felt, and relived over and over in the minds of the Red Sox players. In fact, many of the players themselves talked about the importance of having gone through 2003.

The same principle applies to intelligence operations. Adversity is your performance-enhancing drug. Adversity is your superfuel. Think about that. You need to take the worst of what has happened to you and use it as motivation to learn and grow.

Michael Jordan was cut from the high school basketball team his sophomore year. Repeat that for effect. No need to say more on what happened next. I think he had his superfuel to grow.

Learning from Failure

I was a junior officer and was tasked with recruiting a target from a country that was one of our biggest adversaries. He had traveled to a location where we thought we could get in front of him securely. The target had potentially critical access to his leadership, and we knew from separate sources that he was disgruntled and might want to jump to our side. My operation went awry when I received a phone call that stated that the target had gotten so drunk that he ended up at the local hospital suffering from severe alcohol poisoning. I knew I had to rush there and try to engage him—in this case, timing was of the essence—before he was sent home and we lost our chance at a recruitment attempt.

CIA headquarters was excited. I jumped into a local police car and the officer turned on the flashing lights and sirens and drove down the wrong way of the street to get to the hospital as soon as possible. It was a wild scene right out of a movie. Unfortunately, once we arrived, I was too amped up and clumsily threw open the door and burst into the room. I immediately saw that there were multiple government officials present—to be specific, the leather jacket–wearing intelligence personnel from his country tasked to guard him—staring at me in a way that quickly went from *Who are you?* to *What the hell are you doing here?*

I froze.

I was seconds away from being compromised, and I was afraid their next question would be, "Are you trying to kidnap him or recruit him?" The moment I was about to open my mouth to say . . . I wasn't sure what I was going to say . . . I heard, "Here, boys, take these." I turned and saw my police officer colleague handing out business cards to each one of the government officials in the room. "We were just so terribly concerned about his safety," the police officer stated with a sincere look. "Please call us if you need any assistance; we are always here for our foreign visitors."

I thankfully said nothing throughout the entire affair. The police officer provided me with great cover by thinking quickly on his feet, diverting the officials' attention from me to the business card and his offer of help. We nonchalantly walked out of the hospital; I wasn't sure whether to laugh or cry. Even though I hadn't been discovered, I still failed at the operation, which meant I had to go and tell my senior officer—Charlie—what I had done. Well, actually, what I hadn't done, which was to smoothly and professionally approach the target and seek his cooperation.

"Chief," I said, walking into Charlie's office after knocking slightly on the door, which was open. He was standing up, focused on some papers on his desk.

"Marc," he said, with his usual smile that made everybody feel comfortable around him. "Come in." His open palm invited me to sit down. I took him up on his offer and he sat in front of me.

"Ahem . . ." I cleared my throat. *Where do I start?*

"What happened—did you guys deliver the recruitment pitch? Tell me you guys nailed it," he said optimistically, looking straight at me. It was something that had never made me uncomfortable before, but this time I had big news to own up to.

"Well . . ." I cleared my throat again.

"Spit it out. How did it go?"

The reason I was having trouble revealing to him how the operation had gone wasn't so much because it had ended in failure. It was because I felt that I had disappointed him. He had placed his trust—and the agency's trust—in me and in my abilities to successfully carry out this operation smartly and securely, and I had breached the hospital room as if I were there to conduct an assault rather than a recruitment pitch.

"Chief . . ." I vomited all my words out so quickly I don't even recall what I said, only that I was looking down at the floor the whole time. There was a moment of silence, until—

"Did anybody die?" Charlie asked, his voice steady. I looked up at him in surprise.

"No."

"Did we lose any money?"

I shook my head no.

"Did we publicly embarrass the United States of America?"

I shook my head again. *Only myself, sir.*

"Then don't worry about it, Marc." He smiled, patting me twice on the back as he got up. "And that is one hell of a story that you will tell for years to come. Driving down a one-way street, lights flashing. You barging in like you were assaulting the room. Our police colleague handing out an actual business card to save your rear end. Just epic. Jesus. I thought I had seen it all."

Wait, what?

He wasn't disappointed. He wasn't even upset. He was simply Charlie. Shit happens, I had screwed up, but it was not a calamity.

"These things happen, Marc," he continued. "We all fail at cold pitches sometimes. What matters is that we learn from it and make sure not to repeat that same mistake again. Goddamn, maybe next time do a sweep of the area before you cowboy up and barge into a room of hardened bad dudes."

I got up, looked at him, and vowed that one day I, too, would practice the same leadership style that Charlie had just demonstrated. And, in fact, I used Charlie's famous three questions later on when officers under my command botched an operation or two. Did anyone die? Did you lose Uncle Sam's money? Did you embarrass the US government? If the answers were all no, I'd say, "Relax, take your licks, and live to fight another day."

And yes, I tell this hospital story often at the Vienna Inn, with far more drama thrown in for effect. Nothing like a self-deprecating story among your colleagues to get your Friday night going.

When Failing Really Means Failure

One of my most painful leadership experiences occurred while I was serving in the Middle East, and it stayed with me for the rest of my career. I was running an operation in Iraq that ended disastrously, with the death of an Iraqi agent and the loss of intelligence that was helping us track the regime of former Iraqi president Saddam Hussein. The agent was a good man, had a large family, and looked to the United States as Iraq's savior from Saddam's regime. The agent had excellent access, yet he was taking too many risks in crossing enemy lines. He literally walked miles at a time to reach our meeting sites and had never missed a meeting. He was always on time—we had a set schedule of days and times when we knew we would meet at a specific location.

Then, one day, he didn't show up.

"That's out of character," I thought, trying to push down the sick sensation growing in the pit of my stomach.

I checked my black Casio G-Shock watch—which I wore for several years through so many of these high-risk deployments—and it confirmed he was several minutes late, something that had never happened before.

"I pushed too hard," I told myself, dismissing those voices in the back of my head that told me I knew exactly why he hadn't come to our scheduled meeting. Let's wait and see what happens at our next meeting.

Still nothing. I had arrived at our location on the appointed day and at the exact time of our alternate meeting, something we had mutually agreed upon beforehand, but again he wasn't there.

"He'll make it to the next one," I tried to reassure myself.

I walked away, hoping to see him at our next meeting while trying not to pay attention to the now clear voices in my head that told me a story I was not ready to face.

As the days before our third meeting went by, I became more and more aware of how my body was getting ready to face the facts. My heart rate had risen, and I knew it was time for me to get mentally ready to confront what I knew was true but didn't want to admit quite yet. The day of our third meeting, I arrived at our location and repeated the now familiar ritual of checking my watch: 10:31. I looked around to see if I could spot him. Nothing. I checked my watch again soon after: 10:33. The voices in the back of my head became louder, shouting at me to simply admit the truth. But it was still too much for me to handle. I checked my watch again: 10:37.

No way was he coming. The hair on the back of my neck stood up.

In the intelligence business, we develop a sixth sense where we basically know—we can sense it—when something is off. My sixth sense was begging me to admit what I had suspected all along, the reason why he had missed three consecutive meetings: he had lost his life.

I pushed too hard.

Later, I would find out that he had been intercepted by the Iraqi intelligence services en route to a meeting with me. He was caught and brutally tortured to death. I remember the moment I learned the news; I sat quietly and just stared into the abyss for what felt like an eternity. I closed my eyes and I saw his face, a vision that stays with me to this day. One that I still see often at night, in my sleep. *This* was failure felt. The fault in that operation was ultimately on me.

I learned a damn hard lesson. The pressure to collect intelligence was such that I did not rein him in. And a man lost his life. I pushed too hard, the agent wanted to please, and, in the end, he was caught, tortured, and killed. This tragedy remains ingrained in my psyche and weighs heavily on my heart.

I had failed.

I alone owned this mistake.

I didn't choose to blame it on someone else—on the conditions that day, on the agent himself, on the policy, our rush to war, or any number of other factors. Too often as I look around today, I see leaders who blame everyone else for their poor decisions.

A true test of leadership is acknowledging our mistakes, owning them, and taking responsibility for them—even when it hurts our ego or temporarily crushes our spirit. Make no mistake, our followers are watching how we deal with adversity and if we have the perseverance to do the right thing.

It took time for me to come to terms with what happened, but I knew what lesson I had to learn from that failure: I needed to be smarter and more patient, to not allow myself to succumb to the pressure to collect intelligence quickly—it was more important to do it right and safely.

After Failure Comes . . . Redemption

I was able to apply the lesson I had learned about patience in a different war zone in South Asia, where we were tracking a terrorist that had killed one of my fellow CIA officers several years prior. No joke, this was personal to me. According to our findings, he was planning additional attacks on Americans, so he remained a threat that was very high on our priority list. In this case, we waited months, carefully recruiting agents on the ground to report on the HVT. We were wise and patient and did not rush the operation despite the desire to exact justice and thwart future attacks. On one occasion, our agents reported the HVT's presence, but they lost him in a crowd. Weeks later, the HVT's brother was spotted, and he even looked similar to our target, so there was a flurry of false identifications. Ultimately, no joy. "We will get another chance," I told myself over and over. Pressure to act was immense, but I remembered what had happened in Iraq. We did things right this time, not pressing, not pushing the agents on the ground to take unnecessary risks.

"Be smart but expeditious," I kept telling myself.

As this operation progressed, I continued to think long and hard about the previous agent in Iraq and how I had made mistakes at that time by pushing him too hard. As so often is the case when we conducted our manhunts, breaks come quickly and without warning.

One day, the HVT went to a local market, and we had our agents on the ground in short order to positively identify him; it was seamless. With some later help from the US military, the HVT ultimately met his demise and was no longer a threat. An unforgettable moment for so many.

That night, we made a phone call to the CIA officer's widow, thousands of miles away.

"We avenged his death" was all we said. A phrase that we hoped would bring closure to a grieving family member.

"Thank you," she said in a soft tone, almost whispering.

Just two words.

But they meant so much to me and my entire team. And to the CIA as a whole. We crushed it that day. I received fifty-plus secure messages later that night from officers around the world thanking my team for our actions. We never forget our fallen. And we get after our enemies regardless of how much time has passed. We sat around the firepit that night, beers in hand, and toasted our brothers and sisters who had put it all on the line and never returned. I get chills to this day thinking of the energy I felt from doing something so righteous.

The ultimate leadership lesson from these two operations—which took place years and even continents apart—was that my previous tragic mistakes and the adversity I had to face taught me the patience required to eventually find significant success: an opportunity to exact revenge for our fallen comrade while protecting US forces from future attacks.

A mistake is not true failure. We all make mistakes. True failure is when we fail to learn from our mistakes. This is a universal principle that applies to every profession.

The most effective leaders—the ones people trust and truly want to follow—are the ones who acknowledge mistakes, no matter how painful, accept responsibility for them, and demonstrate resilience in moving forward to the next challenge with greater wisdom.

THE ADVERSITY MAD MINUTE

- Identify a time you have failed. How did it feel?
- What did you learn from this adversity? Did you own it? Jump back on the horse? Make sure you do not make excuses or blame others.
- Identify a subsequent success that resulted from your failure. Do you see how the adversity was your performance-enhancing drug, your jet fuel, that led you to success?

FOUR

THE PROCESS MONKEY

BASEBALL IS A game of process. There is a rhythm to a season, from tryouts in the winter to the first days of practice to opening day in the spring. From perfecting the long toss to strengthening your arm, to the endless rounds of batting practice—which are an absolute requirement to becoming a great hitter—there is a beautiful pattern to a season, and one follows this path for a reason. I think of all-time hits leader, Pete Rose. He talked about how he would hit every day of the *year*, and he did that for his entire life, ever since he was a child. That's a lot of reps in the batting cage. For espionage operations, it is similar, as you contact targets, develop a friendship, and then slowly, over time, gain their trust so they are telling you things that they should not. This was our process. This could take a year of relationship building, but essentially for both baseball and espionage, the process never changes. Trust it, don't shortcut it. It exists because it works. Ultimately, you can't ever cheat the game.

———

THERE ARE NO shortcuts in practicing the fundamentals of the intelligence business. Cutting corners on the basics simply cannot be tolerated in the intelligence world. And there is a rhythm to intelligence operations, where the "romancing" of a potential recruitment target takes many stages, from the initial contact to the ultimate recruitment pitch. Along the way, you are assessing the personality of the individual, finding weaknesses, provoking and pushing to see if he or she is ready to betray their country for the United States. This takes time and patience until you find the sweet spot that informs you when to act. You cannot rush too fast or too far.

Traffic from Hell and Postponing the Meeting

Trusting the process is crucial, especially when you are tempted to take a shortcut. It's not a matter of if you will be tempted but a matter of when.

I was in the Middle East and I had to meet an agent. When meeting an agent in a hostile country, we run a surveillance detection route (SDR). It is designed to enable officers to determine if hostile surveillance is following them.

There I was, on one of my assignments in an Arab country, on an SDR run.

I was in my car, alone, stuck in traffic. Traffic in the Arab world wasn't uncommon. In fact, you might even call traffic the plague of all operational acts in the Middle East. But still, I was on my way to an operational meeting and traffic meant bad news for me.

"Man, it's hot in here," I complained to nobody as I lowered the window, only to be slapped in the face by a powerful heat gust of 115 degrees. I openly cursed in Arabic, not knowing if I should keep the window down or close it back up. Sweat droplets began to form on my forehead.

"All I do is sweat in this damn country," I thought to myself as I wiped it off with the back of my hand.

"Okay, here we go," I said to myself. "We're moving!" My right foot jumped on the accelerator only to slam onto the brakes five seconds later. "Come on!" I yelled more Arabic curses out the window. Nobody could hear me in this chaos of honking horns, the braying of donkeys laden with goods and cutting in front of the cars, people everywhere chattering, and street vendors trying to catch everybody's attention by shouting details about the products they were trying to sell.

"Cumin!" one of them yelled so loudly that it caught my attention. On the side of the road, there was a wooden table filled with small wicker baskets, each one containing a different spice. I was so close to them, I could smell the cumin, cardamom, ginger, and turmeric. Their colors were intense and attractive. Stuck in standstill traffic, I took the time to admire each spice displayed on that table, noticing mint leaves used for the ever-popular mint tea—which, according to the Bedouin, who kept screaming to gain the attention of as many people as possible, could turn a dull day into a successful and profitable one and was the perfect cure for digestive issues. The bright red chili peppers looked so good I could taste the heat on the tip of my tongue. The fresh coriander—

Hooonnnk!

"Yalla, jaash!"

Did someone just call me a donkey?

The heat was causing my mind to wander and lose focus on the task at hand, but the driver behind me forced me back to reality. I checked my black Casio watch and confirmed my suspicions: traffic was so congested that I was going to be late for the operational meeting if I did not skip several segments of the detection route. I had planned for some traffic, but on this day, the chaos of a Middle Eastern city had beaten me. It was decision time. Should I skip parts of my surveillance route—the only way for me to get to the meeting on time? The temptation whispering in my ear sounded so inviting. I was drenched in sweat and dirty. Dust, smog, and animal smells wafted through the window, coating the inside of the car in sand and stench. And the newspaper I had been using as a makeshift fan had grown so weary of my back-and-forth movements that it collapsed.

The meeting was designed to gather important information that Washington was eager to obtain and that could affect US policy. The pressure on me to deliver results was real.

"Maybe I should skip parts of the SDR," one part of my mind said. "That would be a grave violation of our protocols," said another.

The answer was quite simple.

The process must be followed.

So, sitting in my car, stuck in traffic, surrounded by all sorts of noises and smells, and feeling like I was locked in a sauna, I made what was clearly the ethical decision and aborted the meeting. Why? Because it would have been dangerous—if not morally wrong—to put the agent's life on the line before I properly "cleaned myself off," ensuring that no one was following me. And, yes, there was significant disappointment in Washington, yet also an understanding that I had made the correct call in the end, as the safety of my agent was paramount.

Espionage is the second-oldest profession—I'm sure you can guess which one is the first—and this process has been tested for hundreds of years. We know it works, and we also know that not following the process leads to unwanted, often dire, consequences. In our case, the process is in place because it reduces the risk of putting lives and critical intelligence information in danger. It creates safety. It is not economical, easy, or efficient, yet the process must be followed lest the operation be compromised or, worse, we face the loss of life.

In other fields—from engineering to law enforcement—process is also critical for creating conditions under which people can perform safe and quality work. Whether you're a doctor treating a patient, a police officer reading a suspect their rights, or a painter prepping the house with primer, the process must remain ironclad and be adhered to. If we skimp or take shortcuts, the end result is likely to be deficient.

Sticking to the process, however, does not mean there is no place for creativity or innovation or even appropriate risk taking. Questioning standard processes for doing things can lead to learning and innovation and is valuable at the right time—after deliberating and agreeing that there needs to be a change in the process.

Thinking Creatively

How do we know when we're thinking creatively versus just rejecting the process? The best answer to that question is with another question: What is our motivation? Are we looking forward to what we need to adopt as a future practice because we have discovered a better way? Or are we in the moment, coming from a reactive place of wanting to shortcut a proven process to make it easier on ourselves right now?

Let's go back to the concept of surveillance detection routes (SDRs) and see how creativity can be introduced into a mission-critical process. We can agree that an SDR is fundamental to keeping an agent alive. You need to run the predetermined route—sometimes for hours on end with multiple stops—to determine that no one is following you before meeting the agent in person on the street. So where does the creativity come in? Easy. Traffic in the third world can be brutal, meaning that planning and executing an SDR via a vehicle can be problematic. So what can you do to uphold the requirement to be "clean," free from surveillance? Put your thinking caps on in how to work through the problem. How about using a bicycle or a moped that can weave in and out of traffic? Bam, you are never stuck. An officer who came to me with such a plan would be lauded for such creativity. He or she respects the Process Monkey but also found a way to beat the problem at hand: traffic. And they probably got the US government to buy them a new bicycle or moped at the same time!

This key principle, the Process Monkey, applies to all aspects of life, including family, business, and sports. Do not cheat the system. There is always a place for creativity and ingenuity, yet trusting that the process is our friend protects us and the quality of our product—at least until there is collective wisdom on what we should be doing otherwise.

THE PROCESS MONKEY MAD MINUTE

- Identify key processes that are absolutely vital to your success.
- Think clearly about the negative consequences that could occur if you do not adhere to your processes.
- Be sure you have communicated your processes effectively to all team members to ensure that everyone fully buys in.
- Ensure that there is room for creativity, as that will be key to innovation.

FIVE

HUMILITY IS BEST SERVED WARM

THERE IS NO better example of a humble baseball player than Howie Kendrick, who has been through a lifetime of ups and downs in his career. "I'll be ready for spring training," said Kendrick to his teammates after suffering a serious leg injury in 2018. At the age of thirty-five, Kendrick was determined not to let the Washington Nationals down. But luck wasn't on his side. Even after recovering from the injury and keeping the promise he had made to his teammates, Kendrick injured his hamstring when spring training was about to end and was forced to skip the beginning of the regular season.

Then, in October 2019, when the Washington Nationals were up against the Los Angeles Dodgers in game five, things did not look like they were going to get better for Kendrick anytime soon. He committed an infield error—his third of the series. Devastation could be seen all over his face and in his body language. He knew what the consequences of his errors might be: another playoff failure for the Nationals. But he was also humble enough to know what a tough game baseball can be.

If the story stopped there, this would be the last picture of Kendrick printed in our minds. But that image would soon be replaced by his tenth-inning grand slam against the Dodgers, his four doubles against the St. Louis Cardinals in the National League Championship Series, and, finally, his proud smile as he held up the NLCS most valuable player trophy. "All those failures, and even now my failures, still help me be successful," he said. "You appreciate it even more. This is definitely, truly special in a sense that I can appreciate where I came from to where I'm at now."[1]

The remarkable Howie Kendrick story does not end there. In the seventh inning of game seven of the World Series against the Houston Astros, Kendrick hit a two-run home run that put the Nationals ahead for good. Praise for Kendrick was universal as the season ended. Kendrick possessed an amazing sense of humility that made him a favorite of his teammates, baseball writers, and the American public. He was the mature veteran, well versed in what baseball life was all about—success, failure, and staying humble. Every time I think of Howie Kendrick, I think of what humility really means. Perhaps it is understanding that you don't have all the answers. That you should listen to others. That life will throw you curveballs, many of which you cannot control. That you must resist believing in your own hype, even if you are at the top of your game. And that you should never underestimate your competition. Howie Kendrick. I think of him often.

WE HAVE ALL experienced it: the moment of painful vulnerability that comes right after we have told the truth and owned
up to our mistakes. Once the last few words of our confession
have left us, we are met with the most dreaded moment of
the entire experience: consequences. What will the price be?
What changes should I expect in my career? What will my
peers and subordinates think of me? As unsettled as these
questions might make us feel, as unknown as the future might
look to us, and as bruised as our egos might be, this is one of
the most important lessons that we, as leaders, have to learn.

When we are trusted with running operations, companies,
firms, a baseball team, or an entire emergency room, we are
suddenly no longer just responsible for our own actions but
also the actions of those who make up our team. When one
member succeeds, we all succeed. When one member makes a
mistake, we all make a mistake. But, as their leader, the weight
of that mistake mainly falls on our shoulders, and owning up
to a mistake that we personally did not make, but that we will
still have to shoulder the blame for, requires a whole lot of
humility.

Humility is a critical trait of great leadership.

Learning to constructively reflect on and criticize both others and yourself is not easy. There is no worse trait in a leader
than pushing blame down or up the leadership chain because,
ultimately, your officers will know if and how you were responsible for that failure. Though it might sound counterintuitive,
taking responsibility for failure breeds confidence in those
above you. Practicing humility—and vulnerability—may seem

like a trait that is not embraced in an intelligence or paramilitary culture, but I'm about to break yet another one of the stereotypes that surrounds our officers.

Facing the Mistake

During a sensitive mission in a war zone, in which we were assisting the US military with hunting down a terrorist who was a clear and imminent threat to Americans, civilians were unfortunately injured in the operation. At the time, I was in charge of a particular unit that was integral to our counterterrorism efforts, and we'd had a string of spectacular successes for months on end. So much so that I started believing in my own hype and infallibility. Injuring civilians is never our intention in conflict zones. It is anathema both to the CIA and US military culture—although under the Law of Armed Conflict, the operation was perfectly legal. That did not matter to me. What happened, happened, and we had to face it head-on.

So now I had a choice to make. I could easily put the blame on the officer I knew was responsible and seek to discipline him only, or I could take the overall blame because he was one of my officers and I was the one leading the operation.

This event would, rightfully, be a ding on my reputation, as we had been so successful up until this point. Fortunately, I had great mentors like Charlie who showed me what true leaders do and how they behave. I knew exactly what to do. I gathered my briefing notes, placed them in a binder, and cleared my throat.

First order of business?

Take responsibility for what occurred, in person, before the senior-most members of our leadership. With binder in hand, I went up to the seventh-floor conference room at CIA head-quarters where I knew the forty members of the CIA leader-ship team were waiting.

Walking toward the conference room, I took a deep breath and gathered my thoughts. What made me feel even worse was knowing that, at the time, the national security apparatus was under a lot of pressure from the White House to mini-mize the number of civilian casualties in our counterterrorist operations.

"We're going to have to answer to the White House as well now," I thought.

The weight on my shoulders was exceedingly heavy, not only because we had injured civilians—which was bad no matter how you cut it—but also because I knew I had let my leadership down.

But the only way out of the situation was to face it.

I opened the conference room doors, and immediately all eyes fell on me. I surveyed the room filled with clenched jaws and stern looks.

My mouth went dry.

Game time.

I sat down in front of the deputy director of the CIA and the other thirty-nine members of CIA leadership, opened the binder with my briefing notes, and began explaining the sit-uation. During my ten-minute presentation, I identified the flaws in the operation, made definitive corrections to some of our standard operating procedures so that the mistake would never happen again, and never once mentioned the name of the person I knew was actually responsible for this incident.

"Bottom line," I concluded, "this is on me, and I will fix it. Any questions?"

Silence.

Thoughts and doubts ran through my brain.

Why aren't they asking any questions? Are they so disappointed they have no words to even begin to describe how bad this situation is? Am I going to be removed from my job?

Still silence.

I stood up and left the room. As I was making my way toward the elevator, I heard, "Marc."

I turned around and saw a senior officer who I deeply respected walking out of the conference room toward me.

"I just wanted you to know," he said, "it's a good sign that nobody asked any questions in there. It means you explained it all very well and have a plan on how to avoid the issue next time." We shook hands. "You took full ownership, because this is on you. All of it. That's what matters. And you were humble. You didn't come across as worrying only about yourself. And you understand that, in the fog of war, when things go wrong, sometimes the enemy gets a vote."

When I went to work the next day, I received formal feedback from the briefing. Not only did the seventh floor have even more confidence in me as a leader, but my own team also looked at me as an even more trustworthy and reliable leader, because I took ownership, didn't name any names, and didn't throw anybody under the bus. By practicing humility and allowing myself to be placed in a vulnerable situation, both senior leadership and my subordinates viewed me as someone who would always have the team's back, who would always own up to his mistakes, and who would find ways to avoid repeating them the next time.

Accepting responsibility is no easy task, but it's the right thing to do. Humility—in every profession—is the name of the game. You make a mistake, you own it, and you identify what you will do differently in the future—all before your bosses dictate to you what went wrong.

Weak leaders, on the other hand, scapegoat, blame, deflect, or redirect responsibility. That tendency prohibits our ability to learn from mistakes and put in place the steps that ensure the same mistake won't happen again. It works against high performance and continuous learning. Even worse, it develops a new generation of up-and-coming leaders who learn that it's okay to blame others and that it's not safe to accept personal responsibility.

Remember, people watch their leaders.

What do we want them to learn and carry forward?

This is a critical factor to creating a positive culture in any work unit—not just who we say we are but how our culture is reflected in how we actually behave.

Admitting I Was Wrong

I have made many mistakes in my professional life. This comes with the territory in high-risk, high-reward intelligence operations. Yet there is one incident I have never shared. One that I need to own up to that was an intersection between the personal and professional. This one was a mistake I made that had consequences for my own family.

My wife was pregnant with our second child, our son. Our daughter was two years old at the time, and she was into everything, exploring her world and testing boundaries. Family life was great. Then I received word that an agent of ours, who was a member of a terrorist group, had triggered an unscheduled operational meeting in East Africa. This was my guy, whom I previously had handled, and we thought he might have some firsthand information on terrorist plans to strike Americans overseas. The news that the agent was signaling us for a meeting was more than appealing, it was thrilling. I wanted in. I needed to be a part of it.

Being an officer at CIA had always been so much more than just a way for me to provide for my family. It had always been about commitment, believing in a cause bigger than myself, and being part of an organization whose main mission was to protect our country and our fellow citizens. When you have something like that pulling you toward what you do for a living, there is no way you can resist the temptation of being part of a mission against our terrorist foes.

Was there a backup officer who could have traveled for the meeting, who was as competent for the case as I was? Absolutely. This is part and parcel of our system—everyone is replaceable. And my colleagues specifically told me to sit this operation out, take a knee, and stay home with my family. But turning an operation down and ceding it to a colleague was against everything I believed in at the time. Work-life balance was something for "regular" civilians, not a CIA operations officer at the tip of the spear.

"Daddy!" My daughter shook me out of my train of thoughts, extending her arms toward me to pick her up.

The internal debate began.

How can I leave all of this? The operation is crucial . . .

The clock was ticking. If I wanted in, I had to let everybody know as soon as possible. Just as I was about to inform my wife, she beat me to the punch.

"I think I'm in labor."

"What? Now?!" I said, as if she had any control whatsoever on when our son decided he was ready to join our family.

He was born soon after. A healthy, happy baby boy who looked exactly like his mother. Thank God. The rush of adrenaline I felt as I held him in my arms for the first time mixed with an intense joy that I had experienced only once before, when our daughter was born.

"I have to tell you something," I told my wife after the nurse took the baby from my arms to give him his first bath. "I have to go on an operation in the Middle East. I'm leaving tomorrow."

My wife wasn't shocked or upset. We had been together long enough to know one another, what our principles were, and what we held in high regard. She never doubted for a moment that my heart was going to be broken by having to leave her, our toddler, and our newborn son, but she understood that this operation was important and that I wanted to take part in it.

With her blessing, a few hours later I was on a flight to the East African country where the meeting was supposed to take place. On my way there, I had plenty of time to think about the decision I had just made, and I prayed I made the right one for everybody involved—first and foremost my family but also my officers and CIA leadership, who kept telling me that the operation could still happen without me.

The internal debate returned.

*I hope I made the right decision . . . Of course I did . . . This is
what we do—duty calls and we go.*

Days went by and the agent we were supposed to meet
never showed up to our operational meetings. I had flown
all the way across the world and the agent was a no-show. I
couldn't believe it. I had left my family back home because I
believed in this operation and this was now the result I had
to face?

I watched time tick by for hours on my black G-Shock watch,
crouched uncomfortably in a dirty safe house, sweating, dressed
in full Arabic garb with a Glock 19 on my hip. The beard I had
grown to fit in with the locals—so much that I could walk the
streets of this East African country unencumbered—was full
of dust and itchy. I stared at my watch again and again as time
slipped away. The agent simply seemed to have vanished. Later
we learned he was operating on an improper communications
plan and had headed to the wrong location.

Ultimately, there was no joy in the operation. And to make
matters worse, I had gone to a local food stand and devoured
what I thought was a delicious spice-filled shawarma—sliced
lamb meat and French fries stuffed in tasty pita bread. Instead,
I received a truly awful reminder that I was in the third
world—a near-immediate bout of wicked giardia, a violent
gastrointestinal illness that causes immense discomfort and
frequent trips to the bathroom.

Soon we were on our way back home, and during the entire
trip all I could think of, as I spent half the flight in the miser-
able airplane toilet, was having to face my wife and apologize
for putting this matter above our family. I knew she would

understand, but I couldn't help but feel like I let her and our daughter down. Worst of all, I let her down in one of the most delicate moments of our life since she had just brought our second child into the world.

"What was I thinking?" I reprimanded myself.

It was going to be hard, but I knew what I had to do. I had to explain to my wife why I believed the operation was important enough for me to leave her and our daughter behind, why it failed, and what I had learned from it. I wasn't sure what tied my stomach in knots more, eating the contaminated sha- warma . . . or thinking about the big dish of humble pie I'd have to eat when I got home.

I walked up to my front door and, as soon as I stepped inside, I heard our son cry and our daughter laughing. I heard the gentle lullaby that my wife was singing to him and I saw the shadow of her figure rocking him to sleep while sitting in the sunroom. Our daughter was sitting in the living room on the carpet I bought in a Middle Eastern country we had lived in, and she was building with Lincoln Logs from a toy bin next to her, our little engineer at work.

"I'm home," I whispered, trying not to wake up our son. Our daughter ran toward me, jumping up in my arms

"I missed you so much, Daddy."

As my wife placed our sleeping newborn in his bassinet, she could tell by the look on my face that I needed to talk to her. We sat down in the sunroom next to each other.

"The operation was not successful, and the agent was a no-show," I whispered.

She grabbed my hand and squeezed it, as if to say, "All that matters is that you returned home safely to us."

"I'm sorry I left you and our children in such a delicate moment and volunteered for this operation that didn't even—"

"It's okay," she replied with a smile.

Then I walked over to the bassinet and silently watched our son sleeping peacefully, taking quick breaths in and out.

Over the years, there would be many times when I had to leave them to attend to operations that needed my leadership. But I learned a hard lesson from this experience: it is okay, as a leader, to not always be physically present with your team. And frankly, on this operation, I never should have gone in the first place. I had believed my own hype, violating a key tenet of being humble.

Don't make the same mistake. Trust the people who work on your team. Especially when they tell you the operation or project or sale will happen even if you don't join them and you have something even more important than being a leader at work. Like enjoying fatherhood for the second time at home.

I was stubborn and made a mistake; one that was as hard to own up to as when I had to stand in the conference room on the seventh floor in front of forty members of CIA leadership. This time, I had to stand in the sunroom of our home in Virginia, look at my wife, and explain what had gone wrong in my decision to unnecessarily put work before family, vowing to do better next time.

Fortunately for me, both my CIA leadership and my family appreciated the fact that I owned up to the mistake, placed myself in a vulnerable position, and practiced humility.

In recent years, the CIA has been utilizing two management tools that assist with keeping their officers, me included, humble: the executive coach and 360-degree feedback.

Having a coach—a nonjudgmental person to bounce ideas off of—is invaluable.

Similarly, unvarnished 360-degree feedback can shape and sharpen any leader through both a measure of introspection and a heaping dose of humility.

My two favorite lines from the anonymous feedback sessions were: "Marc thinks he knows far more than he actually does." And second, "Marc must understand that his words carry huge weight at the agency, as he is so respected. As such, he should choose much more wisely and fully think before he speaks."

Wow.

I still think about both of these sentiments often.

Humility.

One of my favorite traits in great leaders.

THE HUMILITY MAD MINUTE

- Identify a time in which you faced something all leaders will face at some point in their career: humiliation.
- Think about how you reacted. Did you push blame down or up and make excuses, or did you own the issue?
- Practice humility in your interactions with your subordinates, peers, and bosses by listening to others and asking for their feedback. As one of our senior officers used to say, "You can't listen if you are always talking."
- Consider the use of a leadership coach and 360-degree feedback exercises, both of which will automatically

humble you and give you inspirational ideas on how you can grow as a leader. Both are now common practices that bring out the best in managers; seek them out in your respective places of work.

SIX

WIN AN OSCAR

N 2004, THE Boston Red Sox were down three games to none to the New York Yankees in the American League Championship Series, before they stormed back to win three straight games and force a game seven. Before the critical seventh game that would decide who would go on to play in the World Series, Red Sox first baseman Kevin Millar stood in front of the cameras, with millions of viewers watching from across the globe. He smiled broadly and confidently stated some of the most famous words in Red Sox history: "We have a chance to shock the United States of America."

"What about the world?" Millar was asked.

"Yeah, there you go, we'll shock the world," he said. "If they're watching in Japan, we'll shock them too. . . . The whole world will be watching. It's the most televised game in the world. You have a chance to be a hero. We're going to lay it all on the table. We were down, 3-0 and now it's tied 3-3. We have nothing to lose."[1]

THESE SURPRISINGLY RAW words from Kevin Millar—who was a journeyman player and a true Glue Guy—inspired his teammates to victory that night, and the expression he used, "Shock the world," went viral, becoming a staple of the sports world ever since. My son uses it with his high school baseball team before big games, especially if their team is playing a tough opponent. Before the Virginia Division 6A Concorde District Championship in 2018, my son and I specifically talked about Millar and his brazen confidence in 2004 before game seven. He was getting fired up at home pregame—we have a ritual where we always talk about leadership, expectations, dealing with adversity during the game, and most of all, I make sure he's ready to embrace and enjoy these big moments. He tore out of the house pumped up, screaming "Shock the world!" My boy hit a home run that day, with his team winning the title. Thanks, Kevin Millar. Fourteen years later!

So what really happened that October night in 2004? Millar got up and "Won an Oscar," turning himself into a legend in leadership circles. Millar was in the spotlight and chose to take a time of angst and nervousness among his teammates and turn it into a period of calm infused with tremendous positive energy. He got it.

Out of all of my leadership principles, Win an Oscar may be the most underrated one, yet it is absolutely critical to implement it.

But what does it mean?

It means that, as a leader, there is simply no night off. You are always under the spotlight. Your subordinates are always looking at you for direction. Your attitude can determine the mood of your entire team. If you walk into the company feeling nervous and on edge, your negative energy will be felt by everybody around you, which will then have a domino effect on the productivity of your team. As a result, the quality of work will suffer, causing potentially devastating effects on individuals and perhaps even on the entire company.

Therefore, it is important that you become aware of just how much your mood affects everybody else's in your organization. Think of yourself as always being onstage, with a bright light highlighting your presence to the entire audience who awaits your Oscar-winning acceptance speech. Make sure your speech is up to par, filled with positive remarks so your audience feels relaxed, comfortable, and confident in what to do next and how to behave.

Win an Oscar does not mean be perfect. Everybody is allowed to have a bad day, and it is important for us, as leaders, to accept that we can have times when we just need a moment to ourselves. Often, leaders are placed on such a high pedestal that it becomes hard for us to admit to our own vulnerability. Interestingly, in the teams I've worked with and led, the feedback I've received from the troops is that acknowledging our vulnerability makes us leaders seem more approachable, more authentic. Now, we cannot dwell there, but the point is, neither can we just ignore it. Our troops see it, and more importantly, they understand it. So take a moment to say, "I got some bad news and I need a moment," or "I'm feeling frustrated and need to hit the gym," because it will make you more human and, in turn, more relatable in their eyes.

We are so used to making life-altering decisions, last-minute arrangements, and always being on call whenever something or somebody needs our attention, we often forget to tend to the most important person on our entire team: ourselves.

What happens if we burn out?

The entire team and operation suffer.

Mothers (and primary caregivers of any stripe) are true practitioners of this craft. Their charge is to take care of their children. Yet they find early on that if they don't take care of themselves, they will be incapable of tending to their highest priorities.

This same self-care focus applies to us as leaders. We must be responsible enough to admit to ourselves that we are not invincible and that we are required to decompress. Pushing through the overwhelming feelings of burnout won't help us as people, nor will it help our team members and operations.

Think back to the last time you were on an airplane and the flight attendant instructed you that, in the case of an emergency, you should place the oxygen mask on yourself before helping others.

That's exactly what we need to do when it comes to our own company, organization, and workplace. We must recognize when we are experiencing an overwhelming moment, and we must take care of ourselves before we are able to care for our team members and operation.

Let's agree right now, from this day forward, to accept our vulnerabilities. This is one of the most important steps on the road to success.

Whether we call it resiliency or managing one's energy for performance, it is an acknowledgment that we all have many roles to fill, as a leader at work and our additional responsibilities at home, and there are many aspects to us as human beings—intellectual, physical, emotional, spiritual—all of which need care and attention. In the war zone, for example, my team and I took time each day to do two things to assist us with resiliency: hit the gym and gather to watch "caveman TV"—aka sitting around the firepit at night as a group. We didn't call it resiliency at the time, but that was what we were practicing. Exercise, with its multitude of benefits, appealed to our need for movement, and gathering around the firepit allowed time for us to decompress and to also bond as a team.

Alone in the Mess Hall

A few years ago, I was deployed to Afghanistan and was running an intelligence collection unit. We were rocketed every night, lost friendly forces in battle, and could not even jog outside for fear of the al-Qaida rocket teams. That was the pressure we were under day and night, for months at a time. I led a group of highly trained and experienced men and women from CIA, and they looked at me to always be calm, cool, and decisive.

One day into this yearlong tour, I decided to go out with the special operators, even though it was not the norm for the base chief to do so. I wanted to show leadership that I wasn't just sitting back at the base in a supervisory role, and I wanted to show my guys and gals that I wasn't immune to hardships.

After checking on some of our frontline indigenous units, we sat with the locals and had a typical Afghan meal, which consisted of goat stew, rice, and beans. We were fully aware that we were probably going to get a bad gastrointestinal disease after eating that meal, especially because we had failed to take a shot of bourbon, which, according to urban legend, had the power to prevent us from spending hours in the bathroom after eating local delicacies. We then visited observation posts along the border, and I was glad to share the experience with my team and witness what they encountered while out on their patrols. This was important to me—and important to them as well. I loved every minute of these patrols, as it brought me back to being a line operations officer again.

Although it was invigorating for me to finally get outside the wire of the base, I was exhausted after having participated on this collection mission in Taliban country for thirty-six hours. I returned to our base, hot, dirty, and cranky, with a nasty case of bedbugs after sleeping at a distant observation post, which was nothing more than an old medieval fort with mud walls and no roof. Not even the delicious food cooked by our amazing chefs, who knew we had been out on patrol for many hours, could cheer me up. I cleared my M-4 and put it in the gun rack, took off my body armor, and grabbed a grilled steak. Ordinarily, I would be very gregarious and sit with all my base personnel and engage with them to get a sense of how they were feeling. I would always ask about their families back home, their workout regime, and their health. But not today. I chose to eat by myself in the mess hall, because I was just spent, dead tired.

"What is wrong with Chief?"

"Who is Marc upset with?"

I could hear the chatter around me, but I was simply too exhausted, in dire need of some time to myself, to address any of the responses. My team consisted of US Army veterans of the Black Hawk Down operation in Somalia and former Navy SEALs and Army Rangers who were in Tora Bora hunting Bin Ladin in 2002. They'd be just fine without my usual chatter and banter.

Right?

Wrong.

My decision to eat by myself almost caused a meltdown. Rumors went wild, and it was only because as a leader I was expected—or to put it more bluntly, it was demanded of me—to be rock solid on the outside, day in, day out. There was a perception among them that nothing could ever bother me or stress me to the point where I felt burned out. Clearly, my decision not to sit with them, the first time this had ever happened during our time at the base, had caused them to feel lost and uneasy.

I had made a mistake. As a leader, I was always onstage and my team members looked up to me. They fed off my energy, my mood, and my attitude. I had suddenly stepped off the stage without warning them or explaining why I had made that decision. I forgot to reassure them that I'd be back on that stage soon enough, that I first just needed to take care of myself before I was able to lead them.

Later that night, after realizing my error in isolating myself at the mess hall, I joined my team around the firepit. This was by far the highlight of our daily routine, and all base personnel would gather, often with a beer or two. There I explained to them why I had reacted that way after coming back from patrol.

"I was wrong for not clueing you into what I was feeling and thinking," I told them. "Next time I feel like I need some downtime, I will let you know ahead of time so I don't throw us off our usual dynamic."

Whenever I needed a break, I decided, I would find a quiet spot to decompress on my own, giving me a safe space where I didn't need to self-manage, where I could just be with what I was feeling. Later on in my tour in Afghanistan, I would sit on a guard tower with a book, for an hour each day, to find my alone time—that is, until al-Qaida spotters figured this out and started shooting rockets at the tower. No issues, I just moved toward the sand-filled Hesco barriers and found my quiet space tucked in a corner.

Death of a Colleague

Every day, we hoped and prayed this would never happen. Yet, it is in such times of incredible sorrow and grief that you feel the intense bond with your colleagues. I will never forget the moment I learned that Darren, one of my officers whom I had sent into harm's way, had died in Afghanistan, along with six other colleagues, while running a sensitive counterterrorism operation. While monitoring the operation remotely, we had received indication that something might have gone wrong, and that ominous feeling in my gut returned. Soon after, a senior officer I had known for years called me on a secure line.

"Marc, sit down. There's something I have to tell you that is going to be very hard." I held my breath. "They are all gone."

These words haunt me to this day. It is simply not what we expect to happen to frontline intelligence personnel at the tip of the spear.

I didn't even have time to absorb the news because he quickly noted, "As hard as this is for you personally, you're going to have to find your inner strength because you're going to have to stand up in front of everybody and break the news. It is how you do this right now that will define how every single person in that room is going to both react and recover from this. Be honest with them, tell them what happened, and reassure them that we will get through it. But you gotta dig deep, Marc. It won't be easy, and all eyes will be on you. Now go lead."

In a state of near disbelief, struggling to breathe, I made my way to our conference room.

Having to stand up in front of all my officers and break the news was brutal. I will never forget the howls of one officer when she learned of her friend's death. It was awful and gut wrenching, and it is almost impossible for me to speak of this incident without breaking down. To be honest, I don't recall exactly what I said to them. I don't remember the words I used. But the day after, several officers came to me thanking me for the way I had approached this exceedingly delicate and emotional situation, telling me that what I said was exactly what they needed to hear in that moment. As glad as I was that I had apparently verbalized it correctly, it had been such a traumatic event and I had so much to do in my leadership role that I didn't sleep, eat, or drink for forty-eight hours straight. I collapsed with dehydration and a bad case of kidney stones soon after, which required an overnight trip to the ER in a Middle Eastern hospital, the last place I needed to be. While recovering, all I could think of was that, because I hadn't taken care of myself, putting my metaphorical oxygen mask on first, I couldn't be there for my officers when they needed me the most.

Such an event never leaves your heart. To this day I have feelings of intense guilt. I was in a position of responsibility for the operation, and I can think of multiple ways in which I had personally failed. Years later, when I received a promotion to the senior intelligence service ranks, my first thought was, I did not deserve this honor. I lost someone under my command.

The outpouring of love and affection that the agency cadre showed to the officer's family, which continues still, was what enabled all of us to cope with the tragic event. We promised to never forget the officer's family, offering both emotional and material support as they rebuilt their lives. I hope we have lived up to that promise.

I later spoke of my difficulty with losing an officer to a former deputy chief of the US military's Central Command.

"I deal with such emotions on an industrial scale," he said somberly.

About as sobering a comment about our last eighteen years at war as I could have ever imagined.

Under Attack

During one of my postings to a Middle Eastern country—where I had moved with my family to serve as the deputy of our facility—we suffered a terrorist assault that almost ended in calamity. We had been on high alert for several months. We had warnings that al-Qaida was planning an attack but did not know any specifics. Nothing could have prepared us for what actually happened. Our office was relatively small, and my boss was a former Navy SEAL with whom I had already served in Iraq, under some adverse conditions living in the mountains before the invasion in 2003. We had formed an incredible bond over several years, become great friends, and trusted each other completely. I have not known a finer officer.

As I was in the kitchenette making our morning pot of coffee, automatic weapons fire erupted just outside our walls, and we could feel the concussion of grenades hitting the building as well. We heard the Marines call out on the intercom that we were under attack. Al-Qaida had finally chosen its time and place to hit us.

I ran to find my boss, who was in his office. We had a plan in place with set procedures, from safeguarding our officers to burning down classified material. First order of business was to open the weapons safe. I tried to get my breathing under control as I spun the dial, with my heart rate shooting from about zero to a hundred in seconds.

"Goddamnit!" I looked up and one officer was looking at me as if to say, "Hey, anytime now, boss."

"Are you kidding me?" I thought to myself. "Breathe, breathe." I continued to fumble away at the combination dial.

"Get under your desks!" I shouted to our officers. "You and you." I pointed. "You're in charge of repelling any breaches of the front and back doors to our office."

My boss was alerting our sister facilities in the region that we were under duress, in the event that they, too, faced danger and also to warn that we may need assistance. *Fast.*

When I was finally able to open the safe, I grabbed the weapons and handed them out to our officers. We also had all the officers don body armor, which they'd been storing by their desks since the threat level had increased several months prior. A US Army officer who worked in the office nearby banged on our door, and yelled that they, too, were breaking out their weapons in anticipation of the terrorists entering the compound. As if this were not bad enough, a truck laden with explosives then crashed into the back gate. Amazingly, it failed to detonate. If it had, the building would have collapsed, which meant instant death for all of us.

Outside the building, the local security forces were battling it out with the al-Qaida members. In the midst of this chaos, my boss—the former Navy SEAL—who was as tough an intelligence officer as they make 'em, looked at me and said with a wry smile, "Hey, this may not turn out so well." We had been together for so long that, despite the gunfire and explosions and utter chaos surrounding us, I smiled.

To be honest, I thought this was it. Under attack on all fronts, I was fairly sure we were all going to die. It was just another in a long line of incidents when I thought of my family, my wife and my children, and came to terms with the fact that my time was up.

Yet, we survived. The local security forces repelled the attack. The truck bomb never detonated. Lady Luck was on our side. No other way to describe it.

When it was all over, we conducted an internal after-action review to find out what we had done right and what we had done wrong, all in the hope of being even more prepared in the event of future attacks.

Life is tough in the Middle East for CIA, and things can always get sporty at any moment. This was not the first or the last time that CIA facilities would be hit. Interestingly, my officers told me how much my demeanor helped them stay calm.

"Your voice didn't crack, and you were in control of your emotions," they said. "You clearly instructed us on what to do and kept your tone steady."

What?

I was shocked to hear that. I don't remember the story this way at all, not one bit of it, because the way I felt on the inside clearly did not mirror the way I reacted on the outside. I was flat-out terrified. My heart was racing; I could feel the blood pulsing through my veins. But I was relieved to know that, under such unimaginable pressure, I was able to hold it together and act calm in a situation that was damn petrifying to all of us.

You know what I did that night?

I kissed my wife and kids at home and ordered a pizza for dinner. Then, I was right back on the streets, going out to an agent meeting. There was work to be done—that's just what our ethos was.

My kids laugh at this story now, as none of their friends have fathers who can say, "Yeah, I was attacked by terrorists today, but I need to go back to work tonight. Hurry up, let's go, people, pass the pepperoni, gotta run soon . . ."

Win an Oscar

The key takeaway from this chapter is that it is okay for a leader to show vulnerability. It is the healthiest and most important thing to do, not only for your team members but also for yourself. The CIA has been taking great steps toward fostering and encouraging self-care in recent years, including allowing a few hours a week to be allotted as gym time and offering courses on mindfulness, nutrition, and general health. As leaders, we have to be mindful that our reactions and the way we engage our employees can have significant repercussions on our team members.

There is, however, a fine line between having the vulnerability to admit that you're facing a challenge and unleashing a pervasive negative energy that makes staff feel anxious or unsafe. We are real human beings, and it's okay—even admirable—to share with your staff that you are facing a tough challenge, that you're struggling a bit but are confident that the team will succeed. It's another thing entirely to stomp into the team meeting unable to self-manage the emotions swirling inside you.

Now, a word of caution: be careful not to lean on your subordinates. While it is healthy to show vulnerability, you cannot express to your subordinates that you doubt your leadership skills. If you have a question or concern, talk to somebody in your leadership chain. Seek advice from those above you, particularly those who have more experience than you. If you don't have access to a superior, supervisor, or trusted friend to deeply confide in, still don't go to a subordinate. Get a dog.

Emotional intelligence is a key to successful leadership. It signifies that, as leaders, we are aware of our own emotions as well as those of others, and we are able to communicate our feelings in a safe, appropriate, and productive way. In the end, we set the tone for the team, and our emotions are highly contagious. So it's critical that we are intentional about what tone we want to set—and behave appropriately.

Ultimately, the real lesson of this chapter is that you are always onstage as a leader, and your employees will feed off of all of your energy and emotions, both positive and negative. Should a baseball pitcher who gives up a home run return to the dugout and slam his glove down and destroy the watercooler? Would that help the team? Never. Should an advertising executive who just lost a big ad campaign return to the ad agency and pitch a fit? Absolutely not, as that negativity will be highly contagious.

So, win that Oscar.

THE WIN AN OSCAR MAD MINUTE

- Identify a time when you showed weakness or less than stellar leadership in front of your employees.
- How did they react? What effect did it have on your work unit?
- Identify a time in which you Won an Oscar. What were the circumstances?
- Make sure to remind yourself each day of the necessity of always winning an Oscar. You never have a day off as a leader.

SEVEN

FAMILY VALUES

T HAD MADE HIS baseball debut one day in March 2019, in a plastic bag with a zip tie. He was an ordinary betta fish, purchased for under twenty dollars at a local pet store. He swam happily in the dugout as the Madison Warhawks High School baseball team ripped off another win. Each player came by and gave Thad a greeting, pregame and postgame. Ordinarily, the team drew 150–500 fans or so, pretty big crowds for high school baseball, and there was much interest in the stands as word of the new mascot reached the highly amused parents. I even walked over to get a look at Thad. What the hell was up with this fish? I tweeted out a picture of this curious creature soon after, and my several thousand followers probably thought I had gone crazy. This betta—which later in the month ended up traveling via van some one thousand miles from Virginia to

South Carolina and back—was on hand when the Warhawks won the prestigious Hanahan Spring Break Baseball tournament in Charleston, South Carolina. They were ranked in the top twenty in the state of Virginia and flying high. Was Thad the reason? Of course not. But Thad represented something far more important.

Baseball yet again brings to the forefront one of my key principles of leadership. This time, it is an oft-used phrase, *family values*. It's about sharing a bond and belonging to something bigger than yourself. It's about rallying around a group of men and women who share a common goal and purpose.

Truth be told, Thad was only the beginning of crazy baseball traditions for the Washington, DC, area. The "Baby Shark" song and mascot alike were embraced by Major League Baseball's Washington Nationals in their 2019 World Series run. Backup outfielder Gerardo Parra brought the song to Nats Park as a nod to his two-year-old daughter. It became his own personal anthem and only grew from there, with fans singing the song each time he came up to bat, the players mimicking a biting shark whenever anyone got on base, and T-shirts and Baby Shark costumes filling the stands.

Baseball, Thad, and Baby Shark. Family values reigned supreme in the DC area in 2019.

FAMILY VALUES IS my favorite leadership principle to employ and a critical one at that. When what you do for a living is not a nine-to-five job but instead a way of life, as the CIA was to me, it is only natural that your work family becomes a major part of your entire life. Through the years,

I learned just how important it was for my officers to know that I cared about them and about what was going on in their lives—which is why I made it a point, especially when we were handling a highly stressful operation, to ask them how their family life was going or how they felt about a certain situation. I wanted them to know that, even though I was counting on them as highly trained CIA officers, I never forgot the human being behind that title. Acknowledging their personal struggles and validating their emotions brought us closer together as a team and made a difference when it came to them trusting me and relying on me to make the best decision for us.

Something else I learned through the years is that no matter how much I tried to shelter my family from the stressors of my life as a CIA officer, there were things that had become so ingrained in my behavior and personality that they started merging into my family life as well. I first began noticing just how effortlessly and amusingly my professional life was colliding with my family life when my children—even though they were young—started mimicking the behavior of a CIA officer or inquiring about what they believed my work entailed.

We were living in a Middle Eastern country when my wife noticed our daughter behaving in a remarkably familiar way.

"Marc," she called, "come here and see what she's doing."

I stood close to her and began watching our daughter. She was sitting cross-legged outside on the outdoor patio of our apartment, scribbling on a piece of paper she had on her lap. We grew even more curious as to what exactly she was doing when we noticed that she kept looking at the cars as they drove by, then quickly wrote something on her notepad.

"Wait," I whispered to my wife. "Could she—?"

"Yep, I think she is," my wife said.

We looked at each other in disbelief, and my wife said, "Oh no, look at what we created!"

Our daughter was writing down license plate numbers. Fifty to sixty of them as cars passed by. This is something that a CIA officer would do when conducting countersurveillance, mainly to determine if someone was following them, checking to see if the same vehicle was passing by multiple times. Our daughter must have watched one too many spy movies with me over the years, or perhaps even heard a discussion about surveillance detection around the dinner table. She always smiles when we recall this story.

Our son also showed signs of internalizing typical CIA officer behavior—and lingo—early on, growing increasingly curious of the many facets of my job. He was twelve when he decided to finally ask a question that I suspect he had been pondering about for a while.

My wife was sitting on the couch in our living room, her feet resting on the beautiful Persian rug we brought back from one of our many trips to the Middle East. She was in the process of choosing a recipe from among three Middle Eastern cookbooks, looking for something exotic from our past assignments that she could prepare. It looked like nothing except a normal day in the life of a typical American family. Suddenly, our son stepped into the living room looking like he was on a mission: chin help up high, back straight, serious look on his face. My wife looked at him and smiled, returning to her cookbooks.

"Mom," our son asked in a straightforward manner, "do we torture people?"

My wife slowly placed the three books one on top of the other on the end table next to her, took off her glasses, and looked up at him.

"Excuse me?"

"Well, you know, when Dad goes to Afghanistan or Iraq and asks questions to people and they reveal stuff . . . do we torture them?"

"No," she replied with a reassuring smile. "It's called Enhanced Interrogation Techniques, by the way. We don't torture anyone. And Dad is not involved in that stuff anyhow."

"Okay," he replied, seemingly satisfied with the answer. He made a slight turn as if to go back to his room but then quickly turned around, took a deep breath, and asked, "Did we drone anybody today?"

My wife, who was now walking to the cupboard to start picking out ingredients, looked back at him, puzzled.

"Where is our son getting all this information from? Did he overhear something? Did his friends mention something to him? Has he been looking up things online?"

After many years of working with a highly dependable team, what was her answer?

"Go ask your father!"

And when my son came scurrying over to me, well, it was just too good an opportunity to pass up.

"Did we drone anybody today?" I asked, repeating his question, looking to the ceiling inquisitively, scratching my chin in thought. "Four or five, I can't remember," I replied matter-of-factly. "Anything else you want to know, James Bond?" He shook his head, wide eyed, and retreated to his room.

These little family vignettes still make us smile. And we often remind one another of them. Like the time I called home via a Thuraya satellite phone from the tarmac of Baghdad International Airport, after not having showered for six weeks and sleeping very little, just to see how our daughter's basketball game went. Or the time I watched our son's peewee football game via Skype, with my wife holding up her iPhone from Waters Field in Vienna, Virginia, and me on my computer from a remote base in South Asia. No matter. When our son kicked an extra point, I cheered like crazy, just as if I were there in person, as the ball sailed through the uprights.

Indeed, when your work is so much more than just a job, it's only natural for your work life to become part of your family's life.

And you know what?

I wouldn't have it any other way.

The Vienna Inn

"Are you sure we are in the right place?"

That is the question I see on people's faces when I take them to the Vienna Inn for the first time—equal parts polite and uncertain smile.

Established in 1960 and destroyed once by fire, the Vienna Inn looks run-down: the white boards on the outside could use a fresh coat of paint, the bricks on the side of the structure tell of many storms weathered, and the parking lot can welcome thirty cars at best—if you manage to avoid the potholes and park where you can find even a sliver of a spot. The inside doesn't look any better: old tables that have been there since the Inn's first day in business, posters falling off the walls. One of the bathroom doors doesn't even have a lock. Simply put, the Vienna Inn is the quintessential dive bar; the heart of our town and community.

I take not only friends and associates there, but I also took a famous journalist who wanted to interview me to the Vienna. It's a no-brainer. I am always greeted by name, I don't even need to look at the menu to know what I'm ordering, and on their wall in a glass case, proudly displayed, is a baseball hat with their logo that I wore every day for a year while serving in Afghanistan.

The Vienna Inn is where I used to take my fellow officers after coming home from deployments, where my son and his baseball team gathered after a game, and where my wife and I dine regularly because we enjoy its familiar, cozy, and unpretentious ambience.

Intimacy is pivotal when it comes to nurturing a team, whether in sports, companies, or governmental agencies. Intimacy breeds team cohesion. If you want your soldiers, players, or employees to follow you into fire, they need to believe in one another.

When you care about what you do for a living so much that it becomes a lifestyle, it is only natural to care just as much about your colleagues, their well-being, and their mental health. While watching "caveman TV" (our firepit sessions) in the remote regions of South Asia, I would often ask my officers about their families back home, their relationships, their friends. These conversations eventually led to us feeling more united and more in tune with one another than ever before.

We encouraged one another to do better, to become a better version of ourselves, and to be more valuable to the team. There was no greater joy in life than building a successful team that would do anything to succeed, both for the greater good and also for one another. Sometimes, I found that the smaller the team, the better.

In one Middle Eastern location, our team grew so close that God forbid someone left their desk to go to the gym, because they would come back to find their suit tacked to the ceiling, their lunch devoured, or worse. Another time, one of the officers mentioned we should get a dog to help on surveillance detection runs and to enhance our cover while watching a terrorist target. The officer returned the next day to his desk, which had been remodeled overnight by other members of the team into a full dog pound, with water trays and Kibbles 'n Bits spread across his area. The "bullpen" would even bark at him when he walked in.

Ridiculous? Yes. Essential? For sure. Tightness is key to forging a great team and very much a key to successful leadership.

The intensity of our bonds and connection as a team was no more apparent when, upon returning home from a Middle Eastern capital, one of my former officers—with his entire family in tow after a twenty-hour flight—drove right to my house in Virginia. I came home to find a rented minivan suspiciously loitering outside my house.

My former officer popped out and said, "Chief, I wanted to come say hi."

I hadn't seen him for two years.

The bonds from a previous tour where we were under critical counterintelligence threat, and where we also survived an attack by al-Qaida, were so strong that he wanted to simply give me a twenty-second greeting. He did so and then drove off. I was deeply touched by the gesture. But not surprised. The intense bonds of loyalty formed in risky intelligence operations remain valid for life.

Foster that sense of intense connection and teamwork in whatever organization you are leading. I once gave this precise speech to a high school football team, and I asked them to look left and look right, at their "Brothers in Arms," one of my favorite songs by Dire Straits. I then told the football team, "I know you love your school, your town, your coaches. But, really, you play simply for each other."

Look no further than the 2019 Washington Nationals. From the ridiculous "Baby Shark" chants to hugging each other in the dugout, they were a team that beat others who had far more talent than they did. I strongly believe that the love that they had for one another, their sense of family, was a key deciding factor in their World Series victory.

Practice family values in whatever profession you are leading and it will create only positive outcomes.

Helicopter from the Border

Several years ago, my mother died suddenly when I was serving as a base chief in Afghanistan. This was a location that a national periodical once termed "the most dangerous place on the planet." A return to the United States would require multiple helicopters and fixed-wing flights just to get back to the capital. Then, additional flights would be necessary to return me home to New Jersey, where my mother had lived. Yet our helicopter pilots, many of whom are military veterans from the special operations aviation community and some of the most accomplished pilots in the world, flew me through terrible weather to get me closer to home. I recall looking through night vision goggles at huge ridgelines on each side of the helicopter, our pilots hovering in between them, trying to make it through the mountain pass. We seemed to be floating in this cloud-covered trap, yet they assured me we would make it through. When we finally landed, I thanked them profusely, and the pilot—in the perfect southern drawl that seemingly every military special operations veteran seems to have—said they were honored to accomplish the risky mission just for me, without any hesitation, as they were aware of my mother's death and felt it imperative that I return home.

"Marc, your mom passed, and we are getting you back home. That's all there is to it. Nothing you wouldn't do for us."

That was it. They wanted me to get home to bury my mother. It was just part of the brotherhood and sisterhood that defined us all. I find it difficult even today to speak about the feelings I have for these men and women who helped me honor my mom. On that day, on that flight in the remote mountains of South Asia, they were my true heroes.

When my time in this war zone was up, I donated $10,000 to the CIA Memorial Fund in the name of my mom. I subsequently received a letter from the president of the charity that stated: "I want to thank you for the generous donation in the name of Jill Polymeropoulos, a most remarkable woman. All of us at the foundation deeply appreciate the heartfelt gift, which will go toward supporting the families of our fallen officers."

My Father and the Director

My Greek heritage was quite important to my family, and in particular to my father. He immigrated to the United States to attend graduate school and served as a college professor for almost four decades. He also had strong opinions of the controversial role of the CIA in supporting the right-wing Greek junta in the mid-1970s—also known as the Regime of Colonels. As a result, saying that he was never comfortable with my career choice is an understatement, given the passionate feelings that Greeks share about the junta. He also worried about our family's safety in Greece, considering the history of anti-American sentiment and even the murder in 1975 of the CIA station chief.

After my return from Iraq in 2003, I was awarded a substantial medal from CIA for my actions in helping catch those high-value targets (HVTs) that were members of Saddam Hussein's murderous regime. I invited my father to the awards ceremony held in our headquarters building. A certain CIA director with a similar ethnic background, whom I had provided with advance knowledge of my father's political misgivings about CIA, subsequently took the time to speak with my father, in Greek and in private, for fifteen minutes after the ceremony. It was highly unusual, and I stood by nervously, watching them speaking together, trying to gather information from their body language. My heart skipped a beat when I saw them parting ways.

What did they say to each other? Did they argue about something?

I didn't know what to expect, but, although I was fearful of what I might hear, I decided to find out for myself. As I approached my father, I saw tears in his eyes.

"What did the director say that caused such a response?"

My father would not reveal their conversation. He just said in a somber yet straightforward manner, "I'm very proud of you."

That was it. He and I never discussed it further.

I later asked our director, "What exactly did you say to my father?"

"I told him you were a hero."

I was taken aback. I don't believe that is true at all. I was just doing my job, at the right place, at the right time, and with a lotta luck. But even more so, I realized how important this brief interaction was to my father. I don't believe this event changed my father's mind about the CIA's controversial past in Greece, but that is not the point. As I recall this story, I ask myself how it would be possible for me not to have loyalty to an organization the leadership of which takes the time to make such a personal gesture.

It really mattered to me, as a son who just wanted his father's acceptance.

Watching Our Children Grow

Finally, and most importantly, I have a cadre of friends whom I have served with across the globe. We have seen our children grow up together. I watched my friend's daughter graduate from a prestigious military academy, and yet I clearly remember times at the pool at a diplomatic club in the Middle East when she was in grade school and trying to teach my young children how to swim. When she graduated, we pulled out those photos and couldn't believe how fast the time had gone by.

I remember our children all together in tears, hugging one another at their diplomatic school after the US facility where we served was attacked. The students were put on lockdown and later described their sheer terror wondering if we had all survived. We did, and now everyone is all grown up with unique, amazing, and sometimes terrifying experiences to share.

I think of my best friend, both at work and in life. He introduced me to my wife and is the godfather of our children, who both look at him now as a blood relative. We have been inseparable since the day we walked through the front gates together nearly three decades ago. I was there for him through his marriage, his divorce, another marriage, and even a heart attack. I remember him drinking beer at my house one day and saying, "I'm not feeling so hot." I naturally made fun of him and forced him to have another beer. Days later he was having open-heart surgery. Instead of taking the blame, I tell him that forcing him to have those beers was what alerted him that something was wrong! My house is filled with pictures of us together—from a boat trip off the coast of Beirut, Lebanon, to our time with naval special warfare units during the infiltration of Iraq, where we hunted HVTs with our special operations colleagues and counted the days we had gone without a shower—six weeks, damn impressive. We have shared huge life events together over the decades. We still text each other several times per day, mostly about nothing.

Finally, I think of a former deputy director of the CIA and his family who have become close friends of ours, and how we celebrate the personal achievements of our children—weddings, new jobs, and college acceptances—even more than we celebrate what we each respectively accomplished at CIA. These bonds between CIA officers go beyond work and are inextricably linked with what we cherish most: our families. The CIA is an extended family, and for the field cadre who serve and live together overseas in some very difficult environments, as well as the headquarters personnel who have worked tirelessly and faithfully at providing policy makers with our analytic product, this bond and the love that develops from such experiences is immensely strong.

A venerable former senior operations officer I know said it best. He described each station he entered as a living, breathing organism. It had a vibe, and you could tell if the office was high performing almost immediately upon entrance.

I cherish this description of a CIA outpost, and yet I take this officer's narrative even further. I believe that the CIA as a whole has a "soul," both at headquarters and in the field. This soul is real and tangible, and it involves all the strong emotions I noted above. The soul is the power of the agency, emanating from the incredible quality of the individuals who join and serve. It is an organization of immensely dedicated and talented men and women who have chosen a profession that offers no public reward or praise. The love for one another remains deep, and it fuels our daily struggle to protect America.

And this, the soul of the CIA, based on the feelings we have for one another, is what I miss most in retirement.

THE FAMILY VALUES MAD MINUTE

- How have you built a close-knit team? What does this trust mean to you?
- Give some examples, even amusing ones, of what this looks like.
- If not, what are the things you can do—happy hours, dinners together, and team-building exercises, just to name a few—to build such a sense of camaraderie and loyalty that ultimately leads to leadership success?

EIGHT

BE A PEOPLE DEVELOPER

S EVERAL YEARS AGO, my son—then a highly touted high school freshman baseball player—was super excited when he was invited to the varsity baseball team tryouts. His competition was the resident senior catcher, and they battled throughout the week of tryouts to see who would grab the starting job on the varsity squad. It was unheard of for a freshman to even be given this shot, so my son was just playing with house money. But, boy, did he play his ass off. He was loose, and you know what? He wanted to shock the world! In my view (of course), he should have won the job, but the coaches—who do know more than we crazy parents—thought otherwise, and he was sent down for half the season to the junior varsity squad. My son had two choices: be angry and bitter or get back to work. He wisely chose the latter.

The senior catcher who understood the mantra of the James Madison High School program—Tradition Never Graduates—began the process of turning over the reins for the next season as soon as my son was eventually called up to varsity to help with their playoff run. Their relationship, which could have been adversarial and toxic, was anything but, and the senior catcher will forever be remembered in our family as someone who not only acted with class and grace but who understood what Be a People Developer really means.

The two catchers worked together for hours each day at practice, the senior catcher always trying to teach, to pass on wisdom, never seeing my son as a threat but as a valued member of the team who would uphold the legacy of the baseball program into the future. His only focus was on getting my son ready for the next season. At the end-of-year banquet when the season had concluded, the senior catcher got up and in front of the entire team looked at my son and stated for all to hear, "I now pass you the torch." It was an amazing moment that my son will never forget. Admittedly, I had tears in my eyes, as I was so proud of my son but even more so of the senior catcher, who exhibited exemplary leadership qualities.

Every great leader must embrace this concept: your job is not only to succeed in the moment but ready the next generation for greatness.

Fast-forward to the spring of 2020, when my son's senior baseball season has been tragically undone by the COVID-19 pandemic that has swept through our country. In a private group chat among the players, one of the underclassmen wrote a note to the seniors, stating that, despite their final year being cancelled, their legacy of hard work, sacrifice, and team-first attitude will live on next year and for years to come.

This is what the 2020 senior class of Madison baseball will be remembered for. Just as the senior catcher had done three years prior to my son. Passing the torch.

––––––

WHAT WILL BECOME of our company, organization, or team when it is time for us to retire? Imagining the company we worked so hard for and the sacrifices we made to take it to the level of success we knew it deserved to reach and then leaving it all behind can make even the most courageous leader rethink his or her retirement plans.

What if our successor isn't up to par? What if the moment we step out of our leadership role the company goes upside down? What if, once we stop leading the team, its members feel lost and lose sight of our goals?

The truth is, if we wait to answer these questions when we are a step away from retiring, we are basically guaranteeing the demise of all that we worked so hard to achieve. As leaders, a key role we have is to train our replacements and develop the leadership of those under us such that we leave the organization stronger, in better hands, and with greater human capacity than when we arrived. This mindset, while it may seem intuitive, is often forgotten or overlooked when we are promoted into senior leadership. Many leaders become so engrossed in strategy and execution that we forget that we are a teacher first and foremost.

Mentoring, developing, and promoting from within should be part of your credo, every hour of every day. Allowing a student in medical residency to take charge during an operation and lead the team is essential if we want that student to become a confident doctor one day. Having an assistant manager take the lead on an important marketing project will eventually help not only the assistant manager but also the entire firm thanks to the focus on developing skillful and confident staff.

In my career, circumstances would often arise in which, because of injury, illness, or poor performance, a junior leadership position would open up. There were always opportunities to bring in an officer from the outside, some with incredible resumes, yet time and again I found that promoting from within the group was far more effective. We called these battlefield promotions.

The mentoring aspect is also key to leadership. You need to groom the next generation and give them opportunities to learn, take risks, and develop their skills and confidence.

As I came to the end of my career, it was fascinating to see a change in what fundamentally made me satisfied, even simply happy, in my workday. Of course, I was still thrilled with successful operations, when we took a terrorist off the battlefield or collected intelligence on a hostile state that helped our policy makers formulate the most effective policies for our nation. This was our bread and butter—stealing secrets—and I still got a charge out of it.

But you know what really made my day? What caused me to have an extra kick in my step coming into the building? It was knowing that I was teaching and developing the next generation to lead.

If I spoke at an orientation class of new officers, I knew I had an opportunity to shape hearts and minds of the next generation. If I was fortunate enough to notify a junior officer of a promotion, I relished seeing the smile on his or her face. And when I decided to give an officer a second chance—somebody who may have screwed up significantly and did his or her time in the "penalty box" and now was trying to recover—I knew I was doing the right thing. I would find any opportunity to pass on wisdom from my decades of service—telling war stories, visiting our training facilities to speak with officers learning the dark arts of espionage, and, most importantly to me, facilitating seminars for family members of junior officers deploying to war zones.

Developing our officers became my raison d'etre at the end of my career. I hope my old mentor Charlie, who did the same for me and so many others years prior, was looking down on me and smiling each and every time.

Acting Chief

In Afghanistan, during my periods of home leave when I would return to the United States only for several weeks during a yearlong tour, I would name "acting chiefs," informally, not asking for permission from our headquarters. This gave our young officers incredible leadership experience, often in high-stress situations in which lives were at stake. We were subject to constant indirect fire attack, and the acting chief was responsible for coordinating our response, including discharging bullets and mortars you can't take back. Serious stuff.

If there were a dozen officers at the base, I would ensure that all of them had an opportunity at some point during the tour to informally lead. This also ensured that there would be no favoritism, as everyone would get a shot at command.

One officer, whom I had just named as acting chief, told me as I was getting ready to jump on the helicopter to depart the base: "Boss, don't worry. I'll hold down the fort for you."

Wrong words.

I grabbed him by the shirt, looked him straight in the eyes, and said, "No. You lead. The base is in *your* hands now, not mine. *You* make decisions. You are not holding down the fort for me. Do more than that. I believe in *you*. Advance the mission. You crush it."

I loved the steely look in his eyes as I was giving him this talk. It told me that the message had been received and he was proud to know he had my trust. I jumped on the helicopter and left, feeling fully confident in his abilities to not just keep the seat warm for me. My junior officers learned far more from getting thrown into the fire than from any formalized training course. I would tell them that as long as their decision-making was sound and well thought out, even if it ended up being wrong, I would back them fully when I returned. And if something did go wrong? Well, just as I explained in a previous chapter, failure is a great learning tool, as long as my officers learned what had gone wrong and what needed to be fixed to avoid the same result in the future.

Fast-forward years later. This same officer, who just assumed a leadership position overseas in a dangerous area of the world, wrote to me, saying, "Your informal leadership opportunities were one of the key lessons I took with me from my time under your command in Afghanistan." I like to think he remembered that jolt of confidence that went through his veins when I told him he was in charge of the base. "I plan on using these same tactics now that I am leading in the field," the letter continued. "I want to give my junior officers the same opportunities to lead whenever possible."

I couldn't help being reminded of that senior catcher and his work with my son. It doesn't matter if it's the battlefield or the ball field, the war room or the boardroom. Passing the torch to the next generation—being a People Developer—is a core principle for outstanding leadership.

What is the legacy you want to leave?

No one will remember your heroics and awards; everyone will remember how you taught them to lead. No matter your technical background or profession, not only is this a critical principle, it is not difficult to practice. For example, rotate a team lead for each advertising campaign, or look internally for candidates for promotion at the auto dealership.

Remember, your staff is the incubator for future leaders.

Battlefield Promotions

Human resources departments in the modern age are rightfully strict about promotions. There have been far too many examples of racism, sexism, ageism, and nepotism to think that, in current times, we can simply rely on our gut to determine who is promoted. CIA has had such issues over its history, but fortunately much of this old boy network is a thing of the past. I have huge respect for the CIA HR and diversity and inclusion field to ensure fairness and equality in how we determine and decide the next level of leaders. That being said, there are some old-school practices that we can adapt to the modern era.

I have always loved to use a key concept that I termed the "battlefield promotion," which can be accomplished under modern HR rules.

I was the deputy in a station in the Middle East, and we needed a chief of operations, the number three in the station, due to a regular personnel rotation. There were multiple candidates, all qualified no doubt, including one from the office. I admired this officer for his passion, his dedication to the mission, and his deep caring for those he worked with. He was a bit junior for the position, but I could overlook that due to other positive aspects he would bring to the table. He knew our office and the country we worked in, and he had the respect of our foreign partners as well. Indeed, he was qualified. I was extremely comfortable with him, and I argued strongly and fairly for this candidate. He ended up getting the job and, more importantly, has gone on to a successful career, with multiple field commands under his belt. If we did not give him this shot years ago, he may have never turned into the leader that he is today.

Battlefield promotions.

Something to consider as we develop our people.

Bill

In May 2020, a man I will call Bill passed away at the age of eighty-one. The town of Vienna grieved, as he was a local baseball legend and a member of the Vienna Little League coaching fraternity for many decades, rising to become chairman of the league, a position he held for fifteen years. A local ball field was even named after him. Bill believed deeply in baseball and what it can offer to a small town in the development of our young boys. He was a demanding coach, but the players, parents, and fellow coaches all revered him. My son did not play for him but no doubt battled Bill's teams on the ball field, as they were always so well coached and a tough opponent. Bill had a deep sense of community, and his volunteer work also was seen on the football fields and basketball courts of Vienna, as he coached these sports as well.

Amazingly, there was so much more to Bill, not known publicly until his recent death. In fact, Bill was a career CIA paramilitary operations officer, serving for thirty-three years in some of the toughest locales on the planet. The paramilitary arm of CIA is responsible for covert action, often working in war zones supporting indigenous groups, frequently in great personal danger. Many of the stars on the wall at CIA headquarters commemorating those killed in the line of duty are officers from the paramilitary ranks, having served from Vietnam to Iraq to Afghanistan, sadly paying the ultimate price. Bill, baseball, and the CIA—together again—with the Vienna Inn as the center of our universe.

Bill first served in the US Marine Corps and then joined the CIA and served in Vietnam, Laos, and Cambodia, as well as having tours in Africa and then in CIA's famed Counterterrorism Center (CTC), the operational division that later tracked down Osama bin Laden. Bill retired in 1999, but his legacy in CTC remains intact today, as he helped form a

specialized operational unit—details that I cannot disclose—
that has been integral to our worldwide success in hunting
terrorists.

What made Bill truly unique was his incredible knack of
mentoring and developing all those within his sphere of influ-
ence. He was a true People Developer, highly respected for
his operational track record that saw him rise to the senior
intelligence service ranks. At the same time, his larger-than-
life personality made him special. He had an incredible sense
of humor that he used to defuse situations, put colleagues at
ease, and also to teach. Bill understood how to navigate both
the CIA bureaucracy and the real-world difficulties one often
faced in the field. His advice, always couched in humor, was
so often spot on. According to his colleagues, in his witti-
cisms and lighthearted gibes, there was also wisdom. Bill had
a massive physical presence, and he commanded every room
he entered, but he also had a heart commensurate to his size.
His empathy for others was without equal. Bill could deliver
a hard message or convey needed corrective guidance, com-
monly called an ass chewing, but he always left the recipient
feeling better about themselves. Bill's kindness was legendary,
whether picking up the tab at the Vienna Inn or giving his
time freely to Vienna Little League coaches and players.

Perhaps Bill's finest legacy at CIA was tied to America's
response to the attacks on September 11, 2001. The paramilitary officers that made up the first on the ground teams that
entered Afghanistan, made famous by multiple books and
movies, all had one thing in common: they were directly and
personally mentored by Bill. It is extraordinary to note that
some of our agency's finest heroes were molded by this man,

and to this day they all speak openly about him as instrumental in both their careers and their lives. Two of these officers ended up as chiefs of the Special Activities Division, the famed paramilitary arm of the CIA.

What a legacy Bill left behind at CIA. And in the Vienna community as well. He was a People Developer in the finest fashion.

Setting the Table

The CIA recruitment cycle to spot, assess, develop, and recruit foreigners with access to secret information is usually conducted by a single operations officer, who will develop significant rapport and personal ties to the agent-candidate. Recruiting agents to spy for the United States is the bread and butter of espionage. As the manager of such operations personnel, I would expect each operations officer in my station to recruit several agents a year. While there is significant pressure on the officers to do so, like most things in life, recruiting agents gets easier the more you do it. The best managers at CIA ensured that junior officers got experiences early in their careers in making the actual recruitment pitch, or what we call "pulling the trigger." This not only breeds confidence but also helps in their annual performance review, which notes whether an officer had recruited new agents.

So what exactly does a great manager at CIA do?

A great manager would seek out a more experienced officer in the CIA station who had an "advanced developmental"—i.e., an agent-candidate who was ready to accept a formal offer of recruitment. The experienced officer, who had "set the table," would then bring in a junior officer to make the actual pitch, the offer of working for the CIA, to the agent-candidate. This experience, akin to closing a sales deal, was invaluable in gaining confidence and experience for the junior officer.

One time in the Middle East, I developed an official of a foreign government, who clearly already knew what he was doing, to spy for CIA. We were in a five-star hotel room, a bottle of fine champagne at the ready, as this was going to be a seminal event in this agent-candidate's life—sealing the deal by committing to CIA. I brought in a brand-new, first-tour, very "green" operations officer to provide him invaluable experience in making the formal pitch. The pitch was made, and the agent-candidate quickly accepted and shook the hand of our junior officer with vigor and pride. These moments are always to be cherished, given the gravity of what was occurring, and a time to celebrate.

"Let's break open the bubbly," I thought. But before I could . . .

"Are you ready to formally sign on with CIA?"

The junior officer was so excited that he asked the agent-candidate again.

A puzzled look came over the face of the foreign official, and he looked at me. I nodded to him without words, as if to say, yes, everything was fine.

My officer then looked at me and asked, "He said yes, right?"

I smiled patiently and said through my clenched teeth that "Yes, we have established a formal relationship, but it is better off if we stop asking him over and over or he may reconsider!"

Later on, back at the office, the station officers made the junior officer repeat, several times, exactly what happened.

"You asked him to say yes again and again?" they asked, laughing hysterically each time.

The junior officer had simply wanted to hear that magic word—yes—so badly. He good-naturedly went along with all the ribbing from his office mates afterwards.

Setting the table. Passing the torch. Developing your people. It is a fundamental part of leadership.

Second Chances

I have talked a great deal about integrity and accountability, fundamental principles I hold dear and that lie deep in my core. Yet what do you do about employees who have conducted themselves poorly, have accepted some sanction for their actions, and then need rehabilitation? We can't fire everybody for minor offenses, because we accept that we employ human beings with all our natural frailties. What would we be as leaders if we do not possess compassion for our employees and an ability to provide second chances?

This can be one of the trickier nuances to navigate within the Be a People Developer principle, as we also cannot be seen as pushovers. When you provide a second chance for an employee, the entire workforce takes notice.

I've had to plot a course through these icy waters many times. In one station, we had an employee who simply rebelled against authority. He was not a bad operations officer, but he did not get along well with his frontline supervisor. As a result, and as part of passive-aggressive behavior, he was perpetually and purposefully late to work each day. I took him aside for management counseling, made sure he and his supervisor had a productive discussion with set expectations, and gave him one choice for the next morning. Come to work on time. Period. This was his moment to prove he was a team player. That he was serious about his job. Yet the next morning, at 10:00 a.m., long past our report time to duty, this officer was nowhere to be found.

"Start drafting the message to headquarters," I told our chief of support. "Pack his ass up—we are sending him home on the next flight."

This was a bitter employee who simply was not fit for field duty. To contrast, I had another employee who made some questionable choices in his personal life. In the field, behavior such as excessive drinking, adultery, or getting into physical altercations is not acceptable, not only for basic issues of decency—we are the morality police—but for counterintelligence reasons. We don't want our employees to do something that would then subject them to blackmail from a hostile foreign government service. So, at times, we are strict on issues of personal behavior.

In this case, the employee had made an error in judgment, went through a disciplinary hearing, and was placed in a second-rate job for several years as punishment. This officer was a brilliant operations officer, fluent in several hard target languages, and added enormous value to the CIA. We wanted—even needed—him to take his time in the penalty box seriously, come out from under this shadow, and jump right back into the fight. I personally made sure the officer was on the up and up nearly each day, and I'm pleased to say he is once again in a leadership position in the field and performing quite spectacularly, back on track to rise far up in the organization.

Being a People Developer is also about mentoring those who have fallen and getting them back on their feet and back in the fight.

I recently met this officer at a café overseas, and we talked about his journey. What made me most proud was when he said, "All my trials and tribulations, including the agency showing faith in me and giving me a second chance, are going to be part of my first all-hands address when I take command of an office in the near future. I'm not going to shy away from what happened to me. I'm going to tackle it head-on and use it to help those under me."

Be a People Developer.

It can never, ever do you wrong.

THE BE A PEOPLE DEVELOPER MAD MINUTE

- Do you seek to formally promote from within?
- Do you provide leadership opportunities even informally? If not, identify ways in which your colleagues have opportunities to shine.
- Do you believe in second chances? Were you ever given such a second chance?
- How do you and your organization deal with employees who must be sanctioned for something they did but will not be terminated?

NINE

EMPLOY THE DAGGER

THE DOUBLE CLAP: a James Madison Warhawks baseball tradition. After every game, the legendary head baseball coach Mark "Pudge" Gjormand—recently inducted into the National High School Baseball Coach Association's Hall of Fame after two state championships and sending more than one hundred players to play NCAA baseball (to include my son)—gathers the players in a huddle. Words from Pudge matter to every player on the team. He calls out those who went the extra mile, both the stars and the Glue Guys. "Poly, heck of a defensive game behind the plate, fifteen blocks and no passed balls." Double Clap. Twenty-five players in unison respond with two crisp succinct claps in perfect unison that you can hear from the stands several hundred feet away. "Murph, four innings pitched, three strikeouts, no hits." Double Clap. "Kyle, web gem at short, saved a run with man on third, and you hit a tank that put us ahead." Double Clap. "Perk, great ten-pitch at bat in the sixth inning, and you smacked a double . . . drove their pitcher from the game." Double Clap. Talk to any Madison player about the Double Clap postgame. They love it. A coveted point of recognition from their legendary—and demanding—head coach, who understood that competition among players for such simple but public praise in front of their brothers helps drive future success.

———

COMPETITION IS UBIQUITOUS. We compete at work, perhaps for a promotion and a higher paycheck, recognition from the boss, or to stand out among our peers and obtain greater opportunities. We compete in our personal life, perhaps by playing a sport, by learning how to cook exotic meals, or by hitting the gym to lose weight or gain muscle and reach our personal record on the bench press. Every day, we push ourselves to excel. You never want to be satisfied with the status quo. You can appreciate where you are and relish your wonderful life, but never give up on getting better. My bottom line has always been that competition is part of our DNA, deriving from the basic human instinct of survival. We can't help but be competitive in almost everything we do.

History itself teaches us that competitiveness has always been a personality trait in humankind. Think of the ancient Olympic Games, for example. Dating back to 776 BC, the Olympics started as a celebration in honor of Zeus, Greek god of sky and thunder who ruled over Mount Olympus. A festival of sorts, the Olympic Games were as much a religious event as they were an athletic competition. From running to combat, athletes competed against one another with vigor and determination for one final prize: a laurel wreath. Deeply rooted in Greek mythology, the laurel wreath is associated with Apollo—son of Zeus—who is often portrayed wearing one. Made of wild olive tree branches, the Olympic laurel wreath symbolized not only victory to the athletes but also prestige, honor, and legacy, because wearing it meant they were that much closer to the divine aura of the gods on Mount Olympus.

Indeed, competition and reward go hand in hand. Athletes knew that if they were to succeed and win, they would receive the honor of wearing the laurel wreath. They trained harder. They ran faster. They accomplished more than their competitors. This same connection between competition and reward is seen in our everyday lives. If we study harder in school, our reward might be a better grade. If we go the extra mile in our workplace, the reward might be a promotion. If we eat a healthier diet and do more physical activity, the reward might be better health. The promise of the reward ignites an appealing stimulus in human beings that fuels and motivates us through the process of enduring the, at times, unpleasant circumstances of sacrifice.

The US Marine Corps has a great saying when referring to tough training: "Pain is weakness leaving the body."

Exactly right.

I am not pushing for a "win at all costs" competitive lifestyle. Remember the Process Monkey principle: you can't cheat the system in order to get ahead. We, as leaders, must never let our competitive streak, which can push and inspire us to greatness, tempt us to cut corners, lie, steal, or cheat just to get ahead.

Promoting *healthy* competition among your employees must be one of the main priorities for company and team leaders. To foster this, we need to remind our team members that the raw results of competition among peers does not determine or establish a person's value. For example, if in a group of graduate medical students only one can answer the doctor's question correctly, it doesn't mean all the other students have failed. Competition among team members is not meant to boost or destroy anybody's ego. On the contrary, it needs to be seen as an opportunity to better one's self while, at the same time, working hard as a team for the betterment of the unit as a whole. Remember the aphorism "a rising tide lifts all boats." It is oft used in economic theory, but it certainly applies to competition in a group setting.

It is also important to foster and promote peer support, even under a competitive system. Encouragement—and pressure—shouldn't just come from the leader; it should also be applied among team members. To receive a pat on the shoulder from one of our colleagues might be even more meaningful than receiving formal kudos from the boss, because it boosts a sense of acceptance and belonging to the team—which can even change the way the group is perceived, from an agglomeration of people working for the same brand to now being a single entity.

When my fellow operations officers in a station would throw an informal happy hour after I recruited a key agent, it meant far more to me than when the boss called me in and presented me with a formal Exceptional Performance Award, even with a monetary reward attached. And I knew that the results of my hard work—the recruitment—were likely the result of my peers pushing me to get out every night, hitting the streets, trying to find targets. Tight-knit, high-performing units at CIA that I both served in and managed often valued peer recognition far more than praise from the brass.

Promoting Competition among a Diverse Team

A word of caution. I once gave a speech on the brilliance of competition to a business group, and a very thoughtful young woman came up to me afterwards and asked me, "What about librarians?" I was still pondering the question when she stated, "I'm not so sure this testosterone-fueled principle really applies to everyone."

She was absolutely correct. I forced myself to dig a bit deeper and think about what she said. Got it. I smacked myself, as I drove home from the speech. In my world of intelligence and special operations, it was easy to motivate a group of type A personalities, but that is not a reflection of society. It was turning point in the way in which I framed competition from then on.

As we foster the spirit of competition, leaders must take care to appreciate the reality that each member of the team is equipped with a unique personality and has specific needs. Not everyone has graduated from operations officer training at the CIA or made it through the selection process for special operations units. Within a group of ten people, for example, we might have the introverted one, the athletic type, the social butterfly, the business-focused machine, the funny guy or gal, and so forth. As leaders, we need to know how to cater to each personality to extract the most out of them. We have to be mindful that while our social butterflies might be invigorated by a healthy competitive challenge, our introverted ones might not be so comfortable with such an open challenge. Asking the introverted ones to take part in a meeting and share their opinion with the group, let alone getting openly called out by the boss, might make them feel as if we just put them on the spot, which could backfire and force them even more into their shell. One way to challenge the quieter ones on your team without them feeling over-whelmed would be to have them share their goals with you first—perhaps even in writing if face-to-face feels like too much to them—and then do so with the team. Customizing this approach to meet the needs of every type of personality in the work unit can take time to get used to, but it will pay off in the end, resulting in a stronger, more confident and committed team.

A great leader manages each person accordingly, mindful of their unique personalities and specific needs, to maximize individual potential and therefore increase the overall effec-tiveness of the team.

Rewarding Healthy Competition . . . by Employing the Dagger

In both baseball and my world of espionage, I have experi-enced healthy and positive competition drive seemingly ordi-nary teams to quite extraordinary success. Rewarding this healthy competition was pivotal to the morale of the entire team and, just as the ancient Greeks would adorn the most talented athletes with a laurel wreath to symbolize prestige and honor, as a leader, I, too, had an object of choice when it was time to reward my officers: a traditional Middle Eastern knife called a dagger.

In many stations where I led, for officers who implemented successful recruitments, we would provide a dagger as a token of reward for a successful operation. We called a recruitment a "scalp," which is somewhat crude, but it did the trick, as officers vied for daggers in their multiyear tours or in a war-zone base. There would be huge competition for the daggers, which we encouraged, as this promoted camaraderie and a healthy sense of competition. Officers would keep them on their desks and joke with others who had fewer daggers than they did. Ultimately, after someone had success in an operation, the bullpen would get excited about the next dagger ceremony. It was well worth the ten dollars—or whatever Middle Eastern currency we were using—for each dagger I paid for.

In Afghanistan, I approached one of our local interpreters—we'll call him Mohammad—and I said, "Mohammad, can you please go to the souk [the local market] and buy as many daggers as you can?"

Mohammad looked at me baffled. The money I gave him was going to buy roughly twenty daggers, and I could tell he was wondering why I wanted to waste my money on third-rate weaponry that was certainly not up to par with the other weapons we carried.

He stepped close to me as if he had a secret to share and in a low, conspiratorial tone said, "Boss, are you sure you want me to buy twenty daggers? They are cheap and will break and won't do what you want them to."

I laughed. With advanced firepower at our disposal, including Predator drones and B-1 bombers, not to mention our advanced optics on the M-4 rifles, why was I so interested in a small, locally produced dagger that probably would snap in half if used for even cutting food?

The price didn't matter; I still used them to great effect. I even gave one to Mohammad for his role as the Glue Guy in our base operations. Just like the Double Clap and the laurel wreath, the dagger was a sign of recognition for a job well done.

Whether simple words from a baseball coach postgame, a wild olive tree branch crown, or a ten-dollar token like a dagger presented for a successful recruitment operation, such rewards can be invaluable in motivating your team to greater heights.

Remember: competition is good.

The Stand-Up Morning Meetings

At some designated time in the morning, whether it was ten men and women in a war-zone location or several hundred in a large Middle Eastern station, I would gather the officers and have them tell me one by one what they did the previous night. In intelligence operations, we work at night, and alone, so the morning was a perfect time to get a feel for how hard everyone was working—from hitting the pavement looking for the location where the Russian military

attaché would drink each night or where the Chinese diplomats liked to play basketball. And I would never have to
scold, cajole, or push specific officers directly, because the
results were straight for everyone to see—you were either
on the streets or you weren't. Trust me, you don't want to be
the one officer who says, "I was at home watching a movie,"
when every other member of the CIA team was out on the
streets, deep into the night. A long and painful quiet would
follow such an admission, and eyebrows would raise among
other members of the team. Perhaps the more senior members of the office would take that officer aside and give him
a quick tune-up. Exactly what I wanted—peer pressure but
with a positive outcome.

This stand-up meeting was also a perfect time to set expectations for the following twenty-four hours of operational activity and plan accordingly. Competition drives your employees
to succeed, and in whatever manner you can promote this—by
Employing the Dagger and the stand-up morning meeting—
results will follow.

Given that this meeting happened every morning, there was
an important element of routine about it that allowed even
my more introverted officers—perhaps not a librarian but less
type A than I was used to—to feel comfortable in sharing
about their own operations. They grew increasingly more confident thanks to the fact that they knew what to expect from
the meeting and what was expected of them during the meeting. This was not being put on the spot—they knew it was
coming. It was being held accountable. If you had chosen to
take the easy path and not hit the streets last night, you would
feel the stares of your colleagues.

These types of expectations and camaraderie transcend CIA and can be seen everywhere from corporations large and small to professional sports. The Washington Capitals ice hockey team would pass out a Washington Nationals baseball team batting helmet to the "player of the game" after a win. There were plenty of news reports with the Capitals players looking goofy wearing their Nationals helmets; it was fun and awesome and actually quite productive at the same time. And the players loved it! The Capitals player wearing a Nationals batting helmet was their version of the ancient Greek athletes wearing a laurel wreath as a crown and the CIA officer receiving a dagger.

Nero, the captain of our high school football team's defensive unit, insists on weight room sessions on the weekend and sees very clearly who does not show when the weight room doors open at 8:00 a.m. How does an athlete get better? He or she gets bigger, stronger, and faster from lifting weights, and if you elected not to partake in this required activity, the captain of the football team would find out from his version of a stand-up meeting.

All said, this overall principle of Employing the Dagger is universal and timeless. The greatest accountability is to our peers, and this kind of healthy peer pressure can be far more effective than anything else we can do to help raise the motivation level in our staff.

Competing against Yourself

A final point about leadership and competition. You can foster positive competition among your subordinates, but it's also worth pushing those who work for you to better themselves individually. This concept—bettering oneself—is something to be taken very seriously and implemented as part of every employee's performance plans. Whether it's learning a new language for a CIA officer—think about officers who learned Arabic, Dari, or Farsi before September 11, 2001; they became pretty damn busy at the tip of the spear in the war on terrorism—or a high school pitcher who added a wicked curveball to his repertoire between his junior and senior years and then gets a college scholarship offer. It's always a wise idea to add "arrows to your quiver." You can compete with yourself and ultimately end up far better for it.

When each team member values themselves and feels valued by the team, they all work together in harmony and in balance for the betterment of the unit. And, as leaders, what more could we possibly ask for?

THE EMPLOY THE DAGGER MAD MINUTE

- How is competition looked at in your organization? Is it embraced, or is it seen as unsavory? If so, how can you change this mindset?
- What is your dagger? Find a tangible reward mechanism if you do not have one.
- Can you effectively use a stand-up meeting to ensure accountability and foster positive and constructive competition? Identify a means to foster a sense of competition and ensure accountability even with the most introverted of employees.

> • Does your work unit allow for betterment and growth?
> What are the "arrows in the quiver" that you can identify
> for your employees?

TEN

FINDING CLARITY
IN THE SHADOWS

MARK "PUDGE" GJORMAND'S mind is racing. It's Friday night in early May, and the stands at Madison High School are packed for the baseball playoff game. The smell of the grill has wafted over the field, and the lines are long to grab a burger or a hot dog. A group of dads is huddled around the garbage can behind home plate, the men subtly heckling the umpire, and three college recruiters with radar guns loiter just in front of the press box. Yet Pudge is laser focused on the game. He's got several key decisions to make and none of them are crystal clear. As the Warhawks manager, he calls the shots, but he also has groomed a group of leaders on this team—in particular, a senior class that has played together since Little League. He has faith in them. He has been a People Developer since the beginning of tryouts in February. There is huge pressure, and his players are physically banged up after a grueling year, but each athlete has bought into the system, his Process Monkey, including the dreaded Friday burnouts and endless rounds of batting practice. Total buy-in. No shortcuts. Still strong after twenty games.

The Warhawks are down by a run in the bottom of the sixth. *No worries, thinks Pudge, we have faced such adversity all year and always rallied to come back and win.* Adversity Is Your PED to Success could be the team's motto after the previous two seasons' first-round playoff losses. As a result, the players along the dugout railing are cool and calm, even though they are down a run. Anise, a junior utility player, is on the bench, waiting for the call. He has not started every game this year but has succeeded in the pinch-hitter role since mid-March, and Pudge remembers the trust he has in him. Anise has cooled off as the weather turned warmer, however, so the decision on what to do is not clear. The team is so deep, there are others on the bench to call on. But Pudge also sees Anise as the ultimate Glue Guy, who knows his role and relishes it. All eyes are on Pudge, yet he exudes total calm. He is Winning an Oscar in front of the fans, coaches, umpires, and, most importantly, his players. Pudge turns to his dugout and smirks at his longtime assistant, Justin. "Hey, are we having fun?" He turns to Fitz, another senior and the biggest joker on the team. "Hey, Fitz, we gonna win this?"

"No doubt," Pudge continues, answering his own question. "You and the boys got this. Party at your house postgame." Fitz gets fired up and lets out a scream. All the players hear this, look at each other, and nod, trading fist bumps all around. These guys love each other, Pudge thinks. Some have played together for a decade. His team is the epitome of family values.

Pudge makes the call for Anise to pinch-hit. And, just as planned, Anise comes through with a single to right field on the first pitch, which ties the game. The right call was made. Pudge looks over at the scoreboard with the 2015 State Champions sign and thinks back to other moments of pressure he relies on for his mental toughness. Five hundred fans in the stands and a banged-up team in the dugout, yet he knows his experience will guide him. The Warhawks then tack on an extra run when Chris "Poly," the catcher, team leader, and four-year varsity letterman, gets hit by a pitch, steals second, and then crosses home plate after a line drive double by Mason brings him in. Poly and Mason, who hit every day together over the off-season, played travel ball together for years, and are now on the biggest stage of their baseball lives. The stands are jamming now.

The next inning, top of the seventh, starting pitcher "Shultzie" gets two quick outs but is tiring. It's time for Pudge to bring in his star closer, Murph, who has been lights out all year. A right-handed hitter is up who loves to chase pitches outside the zone. That scouting report from Coach Carter, Pudge's grizzled assistant whom the players all loved for his tough exterior but warm heart, looms large. Shultzie is intensely competitive—he wants to earn that Dagger—and he tells Poly, his catcher, during a mound visit that he is not coming out, period. They are going to have to carry him off the field. Pudge makes the call. He gives Shultzie one more batter. Two foul balls and Shultzie gets him out with a nasty slider.

Poly sprints to the mound, ball in hand, and the entire team piles on each other.

Game over.

Playoff run continues.

Did the above really happen? No, it is simply a hypothetical baseball vignette compiled from several disparate but real events that happened over the years. But it is a highly illustrative and plausible example of putting together each leadership principle I have put forward over the course of this book—how they build on each other to ultimately lead to high-powered leadership and decision-making.

So what happened here? Pudge found Clarity in the Shadows, using nearly every leadership principle to succeed when the game was on the line. Although it was not clear for the hundreds in the stands exactly what to do, for Pudge, as a leader, it was crystal clear.

———

FINDING CLARITY IN the Shadows is the final piece of the puzzle to successful leadership. It is also the most difficult principle to implement as you are putting it all together to make critical decisions. As a trained and experienced intelligence officer, my twenty-six years in the shadows have allowed me to formulate a straightforward and practical guide for anyone to use.

Finding Clarity in the Shadows is the fundamental and final leadership principle that determines if one is a success or not. It means you have an ability—not innate but learned from hard experience and by using my guide—to make smart decisions under pressure with a less than ideal amount of information. Make no mistake, this is not inconsistent to the

Process Monkey principle. They are, in fact, complementary. You have a process and take it to the limit of your capacity based on the situation, but then you are faced with a decision that will rely on all the other principles to guide you.

To find Clarity in the Shadows, you must feel confident, almost relish the opportunity, to make decisions with your chest out, with boldness, with no fear in less than stellar situations. Like Pudge was forced to do throughout a key play-off game. It sounds almost counterintuitive, but once you are comfortable in this realm, you will relish such situations. I think of the simple words "Send me," a biblical phrase that so many in my old world used when a risky mission was contemplated, and officers would volunteer and rise to the occasion even in the face of danger.

The Operation

In Afghanistan, we were tracking an HVT, a key ally of the Taliban and a truly bad character who for years had attacked American forces, causing hundreds of deaths of our precious compatriots. Passion burned in my heart to capture and even kill this terrorist, and it became an obsession of our base given the desire for revenge and the need to save future lives, both Afghan and American. We had spent an entire year tracking this terrorist, with nothing but frustrating results and dry holes. It drove us constantly, each night around the firepit, always looking at ways we could track him down. Nothing was off the table, and no ideas were considered too crazy or out of the box.

Finally, we got a break. One of our agents on the ground provided us the key signal that the HVT was on target. Ordinarily, we would want confirmation from aircraft overhead or multiple sources on the ground, or perhaps an intercept of the HVT's communications that proved without a doubt that the HVT was in the area. We were meticulous in our tradecraft, our process, but sometimes the intelligence picture is simply not as complete as we would like. This time, we only had nuggets for our situational awareness, as the agent simply signaled that the HVT was close to him. The agent could not provide the physical description that we usually require nor any other illuminating details. And it was at night, so we had a more limited capacity to vet the agent's information. Far from an ideal scenario.

Our headquarters leadership—as well as our US military partners—was highly uncertain whether to launch an operation that would lead to the HVT's capture or death. Our usual checklist was not met. No one was wrong to take a knee and pause; it was the right call to step back and think this through.

I had just finished my tour and was back at our headquarters helping oversee such operations. The leadership of CIA called me in and looked to me to help them make the final call. The target had American blood on his hands and was going to conduct future attacks that put my friends and colleagues in serious danger. We had tracked him for a year. The stakes were incredibly high. After some private reflection but with little hesitation, and most importantly, leaning on the previous eight leadership principles we have discussed in this book, I made a firm recommendation to our senior leadership to move forward. I'm pleased to note that the operation was a success as we removed this terrorist from the battlefield. A huge win for the US government's war on terrorism and for our base that had put so much blood, sweat, and tears over years to track this individual. That night, I made sure to contact many of my former team members. This was special for so many, but in particular for our base. I would be lying if I didn't note that there may have been some gatherings at the Vienna Inn in the coming weeks to quietly celebrate what had occurred.

I reflect on this story often. Colleagues lauded me for the courage to have made such a decision, particularly when challenged vigorously by very senior officials in our organization.

It was actually not a tough call.

I was so comfortable in calmly making a critical decision to act because I was not afraid to operate with less than ideal situational awareness, and I had checked off all the boxes in my leadership paradigm as discussed in this book. Being willing to make—and stand by—decisions in the face of ambiguity or imperfect information is a key leadership competency that drives success. I've learned that you need to find total comfort and clarity in situations when others want to flee.

So, let's break this operation down, using all the previous principles we have discussed:

- Who was the Glue Guy? The list is long in this case and includes everyone who had contributed to the team going outside the wire that day. I'll give special credit to our support officers, who prepped the team vehicles with fuel and ensured that they had proper gear. The team involved in the operation had many

complementary Glue Guys and Gals; just an all-star
cast of role players. Check.

- Where was the Adversity that was our PED?
Everywhere. We had failed already in targeting
him, myself personally and the agency collectively,
for years. We had missed the target so many times
and had so much egg on our face that there was
no hesitation in pushing the envelope, smartly and
expeditiously. I had no fear if my call was wrong.
Except I knew that it was not. Check.

- What was the Process Monkey? The foundation
of this successful operation had been put in place
by doing our work up front in spotting, assessing,
developing, and recruiting a trusted agent, who we
hoped would one day come through. We then vetted
this agent and were highly confident in his abilities.
I had also met him personally, and I believed in
him. No shortcuts in this recruitment. He was the
real deal. We nailed the recruitment process and
validation of the agent, which allowed for ultimate
success. Check.

- Was Humility a factor? Of course. I had experienced
so much failure earlier in my career that I never
believed my own hype, even running a frontline CIA
base in the war on terrorism. Was I a good operations
officer and manager? Hell yes. But I was human, and
I recognized that I made mistakes and always needed
to own them. Also, I was confident enough in my
team at the base for suggestions on how we could do
things better. This decision to move forward was not

just mine; it was our team's as well, as I knew they were pushing for it on the ground in Afghanistan. Check.

- Did I Win an Oscar? I was totally confident in front of my senior leadership in assessing the situation and making the call. I believe this was a major contributing factor, as they saw me properly think and reflect but then decisively conclude that we should execute. I also told them, convincingly, "It is on me if this is wrong. I own this." No doubts. Check.

- Did Family Values come into play? I trusted my team on the ground without hesitation. We had been together an entire year, through times of great success and tragedy. We were a brotherhood and sisterhood, with an iron bond that was unbreakable. No doubts, I would go to battle with these men and women anytime. We were also known throughout Afghanistan as a tightly knit group. One colleague of mine jokingly called us a "cult," as we were so far out on the tip of the spear and had endured constant indirect fire attacks and casualties among our indigenous forces that our bond was recognized and respected by our peers throughout the Afghan theater. Check.

- Had I Developed my team properly? Our lead paramilitary operations officer was someone I had taken under my wing personally. I knew he had the recruited agent in his pocket. No doubts. He was a junior officer, but during times of personnel underlaps, he was the lead paramilitary officer at the base, so I had given him that leadership shot and I knew that he was up to the task. Check.

- Was the Dagger employed? Previously, this officer had received a coveted Exceptional Performance Award—a small but coveted monetary bonus— for his work in recruiting the agent. Just a perfect example of the Dagger. That was the award that I employed, above and beyond a cheap ten-dollar memento. So, yes, the EPA was a Dagger on steroids. Check.

Finding Clarity in the Shadows. Not so difficult to see how you as a leader can make critical decisions and work under even the most difficult conditions when you execute the first eight principles I have laid out.

Just as Pudge had on the ball field, or I had in Afghanistan, you now have the tools to operate with confidence and succeed wildly when others want no part of it. What an arrow to have in your quiver, as a professional, in any field!

When it's crunch time, and ordinary men and women cower in fear, you will stand up and shout, "Send me!"

Finally, remember the words from Sonny Quinn, the fictional character in the TV series *Seal Team* who personifies and bleeds the principles of family values. Upon contemplating a risky mission, he laughingly but confidently stated to his colleagues, "We love the shadows; that's where the fun happens."

THE FINDING CLARITY MAD MINUTE

- Can you identify a time when you made a tough decision based on a shortage of data but also based on your experience and having just enough situational awareness that you were comfortable in doing so?
- Do a deep dive on this event and determine how you may have even unwittingly employed the previous eight principles.
- Do you understand that the Process Monkey principle is compatible with the Finding Clarity principle? That you need to rely on key foundational principles (your Process Monkey) but still be in a position to be creative and make decisions in tough spots where uncertainty reigns by using my principles to guide you?
- Does the culture of your work unit foster this sense of measured risk taking? If not, how can you change that?

ELEVEN

HANGING UP THE CLEATS

"HEY, CHRIS," I call out to my son as he slowly steps into the house from a long day of grueling baseball practice. I can tell by the way he's dragging his body through the hall that the coaches had done their job right—my son is exhausted.

"I have plenty of food on the table: pasta, grilled chicken, bread, Greek salad, Lebanese spinach pies, and lots of fresh fruit."

"Pudge crushed the boys today," I say to myself with a smile. "Good. Only way to improve."

"Thanks, Dad," he says as he makes his way to his room. "I'll clean up for dinner and join you guys."

I know that soon after dinner, his friends from his baseball team will all gather up in our basement, eager to just hang out, relax, and be teenagers. Team bonding. Family values. But not before our usual chitchats at dinner of how practice went, from his at bats to his defensive play. This was part of the baseball ritual my son and I shared for years.

My wife is finally home from work, although later than expected—as usual. She has the lead now, the breadwinner, working twelve-hour-plus days in a high-powered job. It's her time, after all the years she sacrificed for me. She has a beautiful smile on her face, which makes my whole day. As we set the table for the three of us in our sunroom, she tells me all about how her day went and how she enjoyed taking a walk in the warm sun during her lunch break.

"Good for you," I tell her genuinely. She has always been the one to take time to care for herself. Practicing resiliency and mindfulness—current buzzwords in the corporate world and now a part of the agency as well—have been staples of her life for years.

"So tell me, how was your day?" she asks while picking out her favorite drink—kombucha—from the fridge.

"Damn skippy," I reply. "I went grocery shopping, picked up the dry cleaning, and spoke with a journalist at the *Washington Post*. Then CBS called because they wanted a quote from me for some topic they're covering. I went out to lunch at the Vienna Inn—the waitresses all say hi—and then came home and did some work on my manuscript. Full day. Accomplished a lot."

"The life of a retired CIA officer, huh?" she teases.

"Yep," I say, smiling. "How different my life has become," I think.

"By the way, I think Chris will need an extra nutritious breakfast in the morning from now on. You should have seen him earlier, dragging his body when he came home from practice. Pudge was amped up today, state championship team in the making. The boys need to earn it, nothing given."

"Uh, my poor boy," she says in true protective mom fashion. "No problem. I'll make plenty of eggs and that 'green slime' drink you all like."

My wife, who is very health conscious and takes the best care of her son and husband, makes this delicious healthy drink for breakfast in the morning—celery, kale, and lots of other green vegetables to make sure we have all the nutrients we need to make it through the day.

Then, the phone rings. I know exactly who it is—she calls us every day.

"Hey, Alex," I greet my daughter. "How you doing? How's your day been? What part of humanity are you saving today?" I love my daughter's social activism and desire to better the world. So much of this stems from seeing the poverty and injustices from our time in the Middle East.

"I'm good, Dad, and yes, my goal in becoming Mother Teresa is moving along swimmingly." She has such a sweet voice. "How's your headache today?"

My headaches. My own crazy journey around the world has finally caught up to me.

It's been a constant in my life for the past two years.

It all began in December 2017, when something bad happened to me during a trip to visit a capital of one of our key adversaries—I'm not at liberty to say.

In the middle of the night, I was startled awake, with ringing in my ears and the room spinning. I staggered out of bed and almost threw up. The vertigo was crippling, and it subsided only after several hours. Earlier in the trip, I had taken the subway. I wanted to see the reaction of the surveillance teams, who were following us. Perhaps I had caught some bug from the subway that was making me ill. I did test positive for mononucleosis when I returned to the United States, but I should not have been so sick. It also could have been food poisoning. Maybe I had been victim to what I had heard was happening to US officials in Havana, Cuba, some type of audio or acoustic attack that caused serious and permanent damage to our diplomats. I felt I suffered similar symptoms, but after some testing by our doctors, they did not believe it was similar, although I was not so sure that it was not related. By late summer 2019, I had gone to seemingly every doctor and specialist in the entire medical community. Multiple brain MRIs, vestibular testing, infectious disease doctors, allergists, and neurologists all found nothing. But my pounding headaches continued. While some experts stated I had certainly been subject to some type of traumatic brain injury, nothing conclusive was showing up. And I never got better, to the point where I began thinking that I could no longer continue serving as a senior official at CIA.

I could be bitter at our adversaries, but I am not. We all have our enemies, and I simply came out on the wrong side of whatever mine cooked up. I could be bitter at the junior

CIA medical staff. I am not, although I do think that the CIA senior leadership could have done more and thought out of the box in helping me find treatment. I was very grateful to all the private doctors and nurses that I saw throughout Virginia and Maryland, most of whom were recipients of CIA golf balls I would bring them from our employee store once my appointments were finished. They loved receiving this unusual token, and I'm sure they are on the mantles of several doctors and nurses in the Washington area.

I survived several years in war zones, including multiple near misses from indirect fire, and I find it incredible I left unscathed. I have been truly fortunate, unlike some of my colleagues who paid with their lives.

It was spring 2018 when I made the final decision that changed my life. My head was still pounding, I was frequently dizzy, my vision was compromised, and I could not even see common street signs when I drove. Watching my son's baseball games, I could not make out the ball coming off the hitter's bat, whether it was a fly out or a double in the gap. I could not even make it through the day without sitting down in my office with the lights out, the pressure in the back of my head pounding for hours on end. I was frustrated at work, having spent thousands of dollars of my own money on experimental treatments, and I was angry as well. Why me? As I tapped my finger incessantly on the keyboard one morning, I pondered my next steps, both in my career and in my life.

Actually, it was fairly easy to come to a final decision after missing four months of work the previous fall. My body had broken down. It was time to retire.

"That's it," I said out loud. "No doubt." An immediate feeling of inner peace pulsed through me. The anger vanished.

I logged off my computer and went to see my close friend and fellow New Jerseyan, whom I had known for decades and who was now my immediate boss. He reminded me of Tony Soprano, was an operational genius, had more bark than bite, and had a gentleness and kindness that was unmatched in supporting his fellow officers.

"That's it, I'm done. Time to hang up the cleats. And don't try to talk me out of it. Just make sure that my retirement party is at the Vienna Inn."

Despite his protestations and refusal to believe me, I left that night knowing it had been an amazing ride over twenty-six years. I would have plenty of time to reminisce with my colleagues as I entered our career transition program, which lasted several months. The Vienna Inn would see a great deal of me, that is for sure.

And, whatever has happened to me is somewhat manageable now, with a low-grade headache 24/7, and upcoming treatment at Walter Reed Medical Center. I am able to watch my son play baseball. I saw my daughter off to college. And I celebrated my beloved Washington Nationals winning the World Series. I traveled with my eighty-one-year-old father back to Greece, a true father-son bonding trip I will forever cherish. Charlie's funeral was a time for me to celebrate all that my colleagues and I had experienced together at CIA.

My doctor says to lose weight, stop having beers, and exercise more. He's right. But I still go to the Vienna Inn several times a week—good thing they have a healthy Greek salad and serve low-carb beer.

Leadership, of course, is the subject of this book, so here are some final thoughts. I have taught my children how to lead, from my son's role as a baseball player to my daughter's social activism. She leads in her own way, helping those in need and organizing trips such as a recent Freedom Ride from Virginia to Alabama and back, honoring the struggles of African Americans, and running medical tents in Washington, DC, during recent civil rights protests. She is the real deal.

For you, the reader, I hope that you find my Clarity in Crisis principles useful in your line of work. Teaching leadership is my passion now, and my role in public life is both fascinating and, at times, highly disconcerting, given how I tried for so long to stay behind the scenes.

In 2020, I presented my leadership speech to a private sector IT conference in Greece, and the response was amazing. Not only did the conference—and the media—treat my presence in Athens as a "local boy done good," but I saw the principles resonate with smart, young professionals outside of the United States. I hope to travel the world now, returning even to some of the places I served in the past, teaching leadership to those who believe in inspiring and mentoring the next generation. I hope you join me at some point.

People have asked me if I miss the CIA. I loved my job and have written and spoken glowingly about the organization and its role in protecting the American people. I miss the CIA every day, mostly the camaraderie and sense of purpose and drive that we all shared. But this is no sob story. I have embarked on this new life of writing and appearing in the media, telling the world so much about an organization that I came to love. And I strongly believe that these nine core principles of leadership I learned on my own from my time at CIA, and that I have now passed on to you, can be applicable in all walks of life—from an emergency room nurse or doctor to an investment banker, to a sales executive, firefighter, or police officer.

Who is your Glue Guy? How many Oscars have you won? Have you Employed the Dagger?

The nine principles were garnered from the streets of some nasty and challenging places, from real-world experiences that are seared into my memory, and from a great deal of successes and failures, where we saved lives and also lost lives. I hope they are of great use to you, in whatever circumstances your career takes you.

EPILOGUE

FINDING CLARITY
IN THE AGE OF COVID-19

THE WINTER OF 2019 into the spring of 2020 was certainly an odd time to be writing this book, as the COVID-19 epidemic swept the world and we were quarantined in our homes for months on end. It raised some questions as to how my principles could be applied in the current national crisis.

One thought kept me up at night: Put your money where your mouth is. You say you know leadership. Now it's time to step up and help out.

My friends and colleagues who knew about my project actually prodded me in exactly this fashion, asking me to address what stellar leadership would look like in the face of such national hardship. They would ask what my view was on former president Trump's response to COVID-19. How was Congress reacting, positively or negatively? What about our state and local governments—were they stepping up and leading? Were our leaders doing enough in terms of testing and quarantine? Ultimately, for me, this was a test to see if my specific principles were relevant during crunch time, not just for a book or for speaking engagements in the private sector but during a time of national crisis. My friends and family urged me to speak specifically about a blueprint for leadership success.

Honestly, I resisted doing so at first, as I did not want this book to become political. I feared that anything I did to try and tie my book to a critique of the previous administration would be counterproductive. My job was to inspire others to reach their greatest potential.

Of course, as all Americans do, I have strong views on the current state of our country and the former president's leadership style in particular. If you read my Twitter account, it will not be difficult to garner my true feelings. But until the later stages of writing this book, I refrained from tying my principles to what the Trump administration should have done for fear of alienating future readership. After all, I wanted my book to be apolitical—and to be a bestseller! I realize now that this was a big mistake.

Is it possible to find clarity in the age of COVID-19? Can we, together, think about and come up with additional ways in which our current national, state, and local leaders could do better? Send your ideas to me on Twitter or in an email, and I promise to respond.

First, using my nine leadership principles, we must answer the key question: Does the COVID-19 epidemic qualify as a significant leadership challenge that is full of "gray," where ambiguity and uncertainty reign, where our leaders and our nation operate in less than ideal conditions, and where our situational awareness is not ideal?

My answer would be a hearty *yes*, as our current predicament qualifies as "the shadows"—and then some. We are in unchartered waters, with a mysterious illness with no cure that shut down not just our economy but the entire world's economy as well. So let's dive into the nine core principles that our leadership on the national and state level could be following, which would enable them to come up with the smart courses of action that will help us out of the current abyss.

The Glue Guy. Do our leaders in the White House and at the state and county levels across the country have the Glue Guys and Gals required to make smart decisions in such an uncertain time? I would argue, "Hell yes, they do." The Glue Guys and Gals in our current reality are the healthcare workers, the first responders, and the grocery clerks who have put themselves in harm's way, and the USPS drivers and the mail carriers whom I see bravely working long shifts to provide essential services. We have Glue Guys and Gals in droves around the country. There is no shortage of unsung heroes battling this plague. And within government, we have such individuals as well, those whom our leaders can call on in such a time of need. At the CDC, the FDA, and other government institutions, there are legions of smart public health officials who are in the fight. Glue Guys and Gals. Check.

Adversity Is the PED to Success. Our country made it through national crises before; September 11 comes to mind first and foremost. We have faced adversity in the twenty-first century, have faced down and ultimately defeated the threat of terrorism, and have emerged a better nation. We can do this now, as we did post-9/11. Remember the abject fear in the days and weeks after the attacks on the World Trade Center and the Pentagon? We thought second and third waves of attacks were coming. There was palpable terror in the air—both in Washington and around the country. It feels a lot like those times right now. Looking back at how President Bush responded days after the attacks, giving his famed defiant speech at Ground Zero in Lower Manhattan—that was inspiring. How George Tenet, then the CIA director, came up with the campaign plan to take the fight into Afghanistan, sending our teams into battle, many of whom thought it was a one-way ticket. I would argue that, as a nation, we got the adversity piece. As for our leaders, there are many senior officials in the US government who were around on 9/11 and in the years after. Look to them to help lead, as they have the experience to do so. Principle number two, check.

The Process Monkey. Do we have current processes that our leadership could follow to beat COVID-19? We sure do—it's staring us in the face. I look right to the CDC on this. We have published guidelines that you can access on the CDC website right this moment! We have had a process to beat the virus, both in the short and long term, that has been universally accepted by our medical professionals: mask-wearing, social distancing, mass testing, tracing, isolating those sick when warranted, and a Manhattan Project–like effort to develop and distribute a vaccine. Seems pretty clear to me. Also, as circumstances dictate, we must slowly, over time, reopen our economy. If we as a country follow this process piece at the core of what we do and then modify along the way, it will help guide us in these times of uncertainty. The process piece is available, right now, for our leaders to lean on. Check.

Humility Is Best Served Warm. Have our key officials and leaders eaten some humble pie in the past that has made them stronger to tackle this current challenge? Well, maybe not those who were in the White House, although one could argue that the positive COVID-19 tests among the White House senior staff may have scared the former administration into acknowledging that they, too, were not immune. But aside from the White House, some seniors in the government certainly have experienced humility that has shaped them and made them stronger. Dr. Anthony Fauci battled the HIV epidemic for decades, was humbled to the core as he watched millions die, but he persevered, and now we have better treatment options. Fauci does not believe his own hype; he is simply a scientist and public health official who provides guidance and advice. Let's make sure our leaders listen to him. Letting Fauci lead, with the doses of humility that he has faced over decades of public service, is simply the smart thing to do. Check.

Win an Oscar. The daily pressers in 2020 at the White House, which were not successful by any stretch of the imagination, were a firm reminder that the public face of our battle must get better. Americans are scared. And they turn to our leaders in such times of great fear. Former president Trump, by all accounts, did not Win an Oscar. But things could change with the new administration. A US president commands the biggest stage on the planet, and how he or she acts in public really does matter. And look at some national commentators, such as former Department of Homeland Security official Juliette Kayyem, who have been so effective in providing ground truth to Americans. Kayyem's appearances on television and social media have been widely viewed around the country as she has offered sobering advice with a dose of hope each day. Kayyem has Won an Oscar. Our other leaders can too. Check.

Family Values. Did the Trump White House put together a cohesive unit that operated in sync? Was there a shared sense of brotherhood and sisterhood among the various agency heads or the original coronavirus task force? Frankly, I'm not sure of this, as so often you heard different administration officials giving conflicting guidance. So the White House could have done far better. Yet, I would profess that this principle was and is being practiced at the state and local levels. I look at my town of Vienna, Virginia, whose residents have come together, not only respecting social distancing but also offering support to local businesses by ordering takeout, providing meals to first responders, and setting an example of civic pride and responsibility. Our mayor leads us in such times, offering encouragement when we need it most.

Finally, we need to ensure that our political leaders do not exacerbate the already heated partisan divide by making the response to the virus a political issue. The promotion of family values by our leadership means not advancing conspiracy theories, not placing blame on others. We are all in this together.

I think we can agree that this principle applies to how leadership must act in the fight against COVID-19.

Be a People Developer. Do our leaders have in place the right team that they have developed as leaders over time? At the national level, it was mixed in 2020. I would argue that the former president did not always let go and let his team lead; he micromanaged too much and did not like it when any other official got too much press. Former vice president Pence was quite effective, in my view, at the initial stages of the crisis, yet the former president then took over the briefings with less than stellar results. Not all was lost, however. The former president constantly praised his team, which was welcome to hear from a leadership perspective. I would argue that perhaps the former president did not listen to the right people; he let his son-in-law, who was not qualified, take a major leadership role, while ignoring others who would have been better suited to lead. The evidence is mixed to suggest whether, at the national level, the former president developed his team.

Finding Clarity in the Shadows. Ultimately, I see that nearly all of my principles are absolutely applicable in leading and making decisions during this national crisis. I hope you agree and can brainstorm with me further how each principle can be effective. And I can say this in a truly apolitical fashion: I want Democrats and Republicans—and Independents—alike to buy my book and get something out of it.

Ultimately, we must continue to press our leaders to find clarity in the age of COVID-19.

Let's hope they choose to do so.

ACKNOWLEDGMENTS

THIS BOOK WOULD never have been possible without the inspiration and encouragement of my wife, Cynthia. When I first ran this idea by her, she immediately responded with her typical Lebanese sarcasm that, while a book on leadership gleaned from my time at the Central Intelligence Agency was a fantastic idea, she hoped I would not teach anyone about surveillance detection skills, since my sense of direction was so poor! She always keeps me grounded, which is a critical trait for someone with a type A personality. My wife has always been by my side when I am faced with great challenges, and there is no one more upbeat and encouraging than her. She has no quit in her—ever. She has always been the smarter one of the two of us, and so much of my success in the espionage business really belongs to her. Late-night discussions on how to move a recruitment operation forward or how to deal with a sticky personnel issue were the norm in our household. And there is no way I would have been able to learn about leadership unless she had been there to hold down the fort through my many adventures overseas, when I had to either leave for months on end or work night after night in some third world location. She is my rock, my Glue Gal, both an amazing parent to our children and the most wonderful and loyal companion. This book is for her.

My kids, Alexandra and Christopher, have watched my career at CIA with a combination of curiosity, pride, and a healthy dose of fear that I would not come home from a war-zone deployment or from an out-of-country operational meeting in a rough spot. I have spoken at their high schools on intelligence matters and brought home an eclectic bunch of people to our house for dinner, such as Arab royal family members, diplomats from countries they did not even know existed, and even Air Force Predator pilots and naval special warfare operators. I collected friends like baseball cards, in packs that stacked up over the years, which made our lives very interesting. In one story, which is part of our family lore, the wife of an Arab security service chief from a hostile country actually called our house and asked if we could arrange the marriage between their son and our seven-year-old daughter. Our kids were in school together in the Middle East, and apparently my daughter had made quite an impression. We did not accept the offer, but I'd be lying if we didn't consider it for "operational reasons"!

To my former colleagues at CIA: you are the unsung heroes of the nation. Never in the limelight but always in the thick of the fight, our intelligence professionals are the finest bunch of men and women that this country has produced. And while I never thought I would write a book that even acknowledged my CIA affiliation, my real hope is that I honored our profession and that my former colleagues can relate to my stories of camaraderie, loyalty, overcoming adversity, and, ultimately, what great leadership is all about. Of course, I can't list you all by name, as you truly remain in "the shadows." Rest assured, though, that I was humbled to be a member of a truly elite group that is so underappreciated. Just the way we always wanted it, although I hope this book helps shed some light for the American people on the greatness of the men and women of the CIA.

Huge kudos to Brunella Costagliola from Kevin Anderson and Associates, a great writer and editor and an even better person, who was my partner for many months on this project. She also saw firsthand the value of the famed Vienna Inn and understands why it means so much to me and scores of other CIA officers. Thanks to Mel Berger at WME, who saw value in this project even from a first-time, rather clueless author who showed up on his doorstep on Madison Avenue with little else than a rough ten-page outline and a vision. And entertainment lawyer extraordinaire and fellow Highland Park, New Jersey, native Matt Johnson, who helped set this all in motion, beginning at the wedding of my stepbrother, Matt Kaufman, in Brooklyn in 2019, where I probably drank too much and pestered him to help me. There are so many others to thank who also believed in me—from Zach Mullinax, who gave me my first speaking engagements, to journalists I met who encouraged my project, such as Olivia Gazis, Ken Dilanian, and Shane Harris. The media world is something very new to me, and they each helped ease my transition from the shadows. I owe a debt of gratitude to former CIA senior operations officer John Sipher and former acting director of the CIA Michael Morrell, both of whom convinced me that I had a great deal to offer to the general public. I remember that first podcast on CBS when Michael interviewed me and, later, how strange it was to hear my own voice. To some other "formers"—Scotty, who saved my life in Iraq, and Brian, who exudes positivity and the joy of life—both of you also inspired me to do great things in retirement, just as you have done.

Finally, a baseball shout-out to the 2020 James Madison Warhawks high school baseball team from Vienna, Virginia, led by head coach Mark "Pudge" Gjormand and assistants T. J. Ehrsam, Justin Counts, Joe Carter, Robbie Robeson, and Brent Weiss, plus assistant athletic director and former Madison assistant Andrew Baird and athletic director John Keny. The Warhawks' senior year was snatched away by the COVID-19 pandemic, and my son and his nine senior teammates would never get to suit up again together. Yet the ten seniors and, really, the entire varsity squad learned more about adversity this year than most will in a lifetime, and they will all be stronger for it. Most importantly, they are all brothers for life, and that can never be taken from them. It was an honor getting to know such an amazing group of players and coaches, and they all got a full dose of my leadership philosophy. I'll wear my Warhawks hat for life.

And to the nutty Warhawk sports dads—Ryan Novak, Dan Perkins, Nick Yates, Chris Lipp, John Schrader, and Scott Howat in particular—we will always have the garbage can behind home plate to ensure real "home team advantage." See y'all at the Vienna Inn!

NOTES

Introduction

1. *Diversity and Inclusion at the CIA*, A Publication from the Central Intelligence Agency (Office of Public Affairs, July 2014). Accessed at https://www.cia.gov/library/publications/resources/diversity-inclusion-at-the-cia/Diversity_And_Inclusion.pdf.
2. *Diversity and Inclusion at the CIA*, A Publication from the Central Intelligence Agency (Office of Public Affairs, July 2014).
3. *Directorate of Science and Technology: Technology So Advanced, it's Classified*, A Publication from the Central Intelligence Agency, February 12, 2009. Updated May 12, 2016. Accessed at https://www.cia.gov/news-information/featured-story-archive/directorate-of-science-and-technology.html.
4. *Directorate of Support: Mission-Driven-Solutions* (News and Information, Historical Document). Posted November 26, 2008, at 1:00 p.m. Last Updated: April 30, 2013. Accessed at https://www.cia.gov/news-information/featured-story-archive/2008-featured-story-archive/ds-mission-driven-solutions.html.
5. *Digital Information* (Offices of CIA) Posted: October 1, 2015, at 10:04 a.m. Last updated: July 13, 2017, 11:55 a.m. Accessed at https://www.cia.gov/offices-of-cia/digital-innovation.
6. *Diversity and Inclusion at the CIA*, A Publication from the Central Intelligence Agency (Office of Public Affairs, July 2014).
7. James A. Michener, *Caravans* (New York: Random House, 1963), 12.

Chapter Two

1. David Ross, "Elite 'Glue Guys' 101," *Players Tribune*, July 19, 2017. Accessed at https://www.theplayerstribune.com/en-us/articles/david-ross-mlb-elite-glue-guys-101.

Chapter Five

1. David Waldstein, "For the Nationals, Howie Kendrick's Resilience Says It All," *New York Times*, October 18, 2019. Accessed at https://www.nytimes.com/2019/10/18/sports/washington-nationals-howie-kendricks-.html.

Chapter Six

1. Mike DiGiovanna, "Sox Can Ace History Test," *Los Angeles Times*, October 20, 2004. Accessed at https://www.latimes.com/archives/la-xpm-2004-oct-20-sp-alcs20-story.html.

INDEX

INDEX

bettering oneself, 122–23
Bill (coach and officer), 104–7
bin Laden, Osama, 71, 105
Black Hawk Down, 71
blame, 39, 53, 54, 57
bonding, xxxii–xxxiii, 81–95
  in baseball, 81–82
  and blending of work/family life,
      82–85
  and brotherhood, 89–91
  as factor in decision-making, 133
  intimacy and, 86–89
  and organizational strength,
      93–95
  personal gestures by leaders,
      91–92
  and resilience, 69
Boone, Aaron, 32
Boston Red Sox, xxx, 13, 32–33,
    65–66
Brennan, John, xxviii
brotherhood, xxxii–xxxiii, 21, 89–91,
    133, 150
"Brothers in Arms" (songs), 89
Bush, George W., 148

calm, 23, 66, 69, 77
Cambodia, 105
Cape Cod, 4
Caravan (Michener), xxv
caregivers, self-care for, 68
caring, 3–5, 87
Carter, Coach, 127
"caveman TV," 69, 87
CDC (Centers for Disease Control
    and Prevention), 147
Central Intelligence Agency (CIA)
  agent recruitment in, 6–8
  author's career in, xxiv–xxix, 30,
      140–43
  base food at, 25–26
  bonds between officers, 93–95
  and civilian injuries, 54
  Counterterrorism Center, 105–6
  culture, xxxi–xxxiii

decision-making in, 130–31
diversity of workforce, xvii–xxiv
ethos, xiv–xv, 77
feedback tools, 62–63
history, xv–xvi
leadership lessons from,
    xxxiii–xxxiv
paramilitary arm of, 105–7
promotion in, 103–4
responsibilities of, xvi–xviii
self-care at, 78
soul of, 94–95
Special Activities Division, 107
support for Greek junta by, 91, 92
terrorist attacks on facilities, 77
truth and integrity at, xiii–xiv
see also specific directorates
changes, in routine, 69–72
Charleston, S.C., 82
Charlie (senior officer), 2–4, 6–7, 9,
    34–36, 54, 101, 142
"Chef," 25–26
Chesney, Kenny, x
Chicago Cubs, 13
CIA. *see* Central Intelligence
    Agency
CIA Memorial Fund, 90–91
CIA Memorial Wall, 5, 105
civilian injuries, 22–24, 54–57
Clarity in Crisis leadership
  philosophy, 10–11, 143–44
  in COVID-19 pandemic, 145–51
  for decision-making, 125–28,
      131–34
  see also specific principles
Clarity in the Shadows principle. *see*
    decision-making
cohesion, team, 87–88
Cold War, 6
communicable action, 10
communication, 71–72, 79, 82–83
competition, 113–24
  accountability and, 120–22
  to better yourself, 122–23
  in diverse teams, 117–18

INDEX

Nine Line, 23
NLCS (National League
   Championship Series), 52
North Africa, xv
North Korea, 31

O'Brien, Charlie, 21
Olympic Games, ancient,
   114–15, 119
Operation Iraqi Freedom,
   29–30
operations officers, xxviii, 17
Oregon State University, xxvi
organizational strength, 93–95,
   97–99, 116
Organization of Strategic Services
   (OSS), xvi
Orwell, George, xviii

Palmyra, Syria, 14
paramilitary arm of CIA, 105–7
Parra, Gerardo, 82
PAs (physician assistants), 22–24
patience, 39–41
peer support and recognition, 116–17
Pence, Mike, 151
penetration agent, 18
People Developer principle. see team
   member development
perfection, 67
performance enhancement, 29–33,
   122–23
Perk (baseball player), 114
personal behavior, 110–11
personal gestures, by leaders,
   91–92
personality, motivation and, 117–18
Petra, Jordan, 14
physician assistants (PAs), 22–24
politicization, of COVID
   response, 150
Polymeropoulos, Alex (daughter),
   58, 61, 83–84, 86, 139, 143
Polymeropoulos, Chris "Poly" (son),
   113, 127, 137, 139

birth of, 58–59
bonding over baseball with,
   xxx–xiv
confidence of, 66
and intersection of work and
   family life, 84–86
leadership lessons from, 143
team member development for,
   97–99
work ethic of, 15–16
Polymeropoulos, Cynthia (wife),
   xxvii–xxx, 57–62, 83–85, 93,
   138–39
Polymeropoulos, Jill (mother), xxvi,
   xxvii, 89–91
Polymeropoulos, Marc, xxiv–xxix,
   30, 140–43
posttraumatic stress disorder
   (PTSD), 3–4
praise, 19, 22–24, 113–14
pranks, 88
presence, of leader, 62
prestige, 115
processes, 43–49
   building skill with, 43–44
   in COVID-19 pandemic,
      148–49
   creative thinking vs. rejecting,
      48–49
   as factor in decision-making, 132
   trusting, 44–48, 128–29
promotions, 100, 101, 103–4
PTSD (posttraumatic stress
   disorder), 3–4
punishment, 101, 110–11
pushover, being a, 109–10
Putin, Vladimir, 31

quitting, 32

readiness, for leadership, 1–3
recognition, 116–17, 120
recruitment
   of agents, 6–7
   celebrating, 116–17

ABOUT THE AUTHOR

MARC POLYMEROPOULOS retired in 2019 from the senior intelligence service ranks at the CIA after a twenty-six-year career in operational headquarters and field management assignments covering the Middle East, Europe, Eurasia, and counterterrorism. He served in both Iraq and Afghanistan, and he is one of the CIA's most decorated field officers. Marc is the recipient of the Distinguished Career Intelligence Medal, the Distinguished Intelligence Medal, the Intelligence Medal of Merit, and the Intelligence Commendation Medal. His last position was overseeing the CIA's clandestine operations in Europe and Eurasia. He is a respected commentator on foreign policy and intelligence matters and is widely quoted in both the US and international media.